if nothing happens...

The Courtship Letters of Norman Wilson Ingerson and Stella May Murdock 1892-1896

Jennifer Riesmeyer Elvgren

Paul Leone

Chautauqua Region Press
Westfield, New York
2001

*Cover: Wedding photo, Norman Wilson Ingerson
and Stella May Murdock, November, 1896.*

Printed in the United States of America

International Standard Book Number:
0-9658955-5-6

Chautauqua Region Press
19 Spring Street
Westfield, New York 14787

For my parents,
William Frederick Riesmeyer III
and Carolyn Taggart Riesmeyer,
who have kept faith and family well

Foreword

What a splendid history here unfolds.

Jenn Elvgren's voice was animated on the telephone when she announced to me the fact of the letters. "Love letters," she said. "From my great-grandparents. They were picking grapes in Portland."

I am nourished by the history of Chautauqua County. The Gay Nineties, I know very well, were exciting and energetic at Chautauqua Lake. Magnificent resort hotels serviced a flourishing summer trade. Recently completed rail lines encircled the lake, and majestic steamboats plied its waters. Chautauqua Institution, twenty-years-old, delivered an engaging season. Celeron Park opened. Against this backdrop, the word of young lovers promised romance. "How many are there?" I asked, innocently. "Oh," Jenn replied. "About a hundred and sixty."

Shortly after our telephone conversation a package arrived in the mail. One hundred and sixty two transcripts complete with photographs. I approached them greedily. Was immediately gratified with intimate and picturesque detail, with corroboration of life I had imagined in unguarded voice. I awaited the passion.

Norman turned out to be an earnest young man of sober aspiration. Stella seemed somehow distracted, somehow resigned. Letter followed upon letter in interminable succession like the days of Stella's life in the Pennsylvania countryside. Was I expecting emotional professions of love?

There is passion, and there is Passion. Norman and Stella are not yet twenty when their correspondence begins. Through three years of long distance courtship, they only rarely manage to see each other. Their passion is subtle, not tempestuous. Their courtship is integral, not primary to the passionate strains of their experience. What emerges through these letters, and what I ought to have expected, for unguarded voice tells the truest tale, is the fragility and poignancy of life. Family responsibility, marriage and birth, longing and loneliness, faith, and ever present sickness alongside the spectre of Death – these are the strains of middle class, Victorian life. Acceptance pervades throughout. Things are as they must be, otherwise they would not be so.

Marriage was essential to Victorian righteousness. Like birth, aging, and death, it was a condition of life. Not merely for Stella, but for Norman, too. Norman never questions the righteous path, nor ever doubts its certain rewards. Norman would never not be married.

Nor would Stella, although she most definitely hesitates. Limited possibility and lack of control make marriage her only option. She is dependent upon family for occupation. In the event of crisis, extended sickness or death, she is expected to assume responsibility. Even so, she is far less eager than Norman. Norman's eagerness escalates with his confident emergence toward respectability. Whatever emergence Stella might have known is subordinate to duty and the expectation of others. Three family deaths occur in the year before her marriage.

The Ingerson letters confirm the impression of simplicity associated with late Victorian, rural American life. The romance of simplicity emerges like a dream in the mundane and cyclical routine of Norman and Stella's experience. Their experience, however, and their beguiling description of it, is profound beyond mere horse and buggy romance. Their letters confirm the complexity of necessity and emotion that accompanies human endeavor. Norman and Stella are not aware that they are living a romance. Like the best of history, their letters elicit compassion. Like the best of story, they are universal as well as personal. They ennoble a history that, like memory, ever recedes.

Paul Leone
November 30, 2000

Introduction

The old maple dresser stood in the corner of my Grandmother Marian Riesmeyer's bedroom for as long as anyone could remember. Grandmother Marian saved everything, and, over the years, that dresser became the family archives. Shortly before her death in 1989, she sold her house, and my family gathered to help sort and pack up her belongings. Her second son and my father, William, tackled the maple dresser. In its drawers he found almost one hundred sixty five years' worth of letters, greeting cards, wedding invitations, graduation announcements, legal papers and photographs. He piled this inheritance into cardboard boxes, large and small, and stored them at his house, where they lay untouched for another five years.

A winter since while I was visiting my parents, my father and I stepped into a time machine of sorts as we began to dig through the mountains of memorabilia. Over the next few years what emerged was a life portrait of Grandmother's mother and my great-grandmother, Estella (Stella) May Murdock. Stella's collection of letters from family and friends numbers close to four hundred. The earliest is dated 1881, from her cousin Dollie Gray; and the final arrived in 1926, the year of her death, from Grandmother Marian who was away at college. Easily the most compelling correspondence of the collection is a series of one hundred sixty two courtship letters exchanged between Stella and her sweetheart, Norman Wilson Ingerson, who would become my great-grandfather. These courtship letters are the focus of this book.

The letters are beautiful and touching, both as expressions of humanity and as primary source history. The quantity and the duration of the correspondence provide a treasure of documentary detail against which the emotional content unfolds. Both my great-grandparents were born in 1872, Stella on November 29 in Sparta Township, Crawford County, Pennsylvania; and Norman on December 19 in Ellery Township, Chautauqua County, New

York. Both finished high school in mid-1892 and that fall signed on to pick grapes at Southside Vineyard, Brocton, New York. Norman wrote the first of the courtship letters two days after the grape harvest was completed. The correspondence continued for the next four years until just days before he and Stella married.

Norman wrote from various locations in Chautauqua County where his extended family lived in a number of communities along the eastern shore of Chautauqua Lake. He penned the letters while staying in his relatives' houses, particularly his brother George's, which he considered "home." Shortly after the grape harvest, he enrolled at Jamestown Business College. While there and afterwards, during employment in Jamestown, he wrote from boarding houses.

Stella answered either from her father's farm near Spartansburg in Sparta Township, or from her elder brother Irva's home in Dubois, Pennsylvania. When she returned to the farm from the grape fields, Stella was immediately persuaded by her sister-in-law, Eliza, to move out to Dubois, Clearfield County, to work in her brother's new portrait studio. Except for visitations to the farm in the summer of 1893 and at Christmas in 1894, she spent the first three years of the correspondence in Dubois. In September 1895, she returned to the farm where she remained until her marriage fourteen months later.

The courtship, then, evolved in four distinct locations–Chautauqua Lake and Jamestown, Dubois and the Sparta farm. The accumulated letters vividly describe each of the settings. Filtered through the consciousness of Norman and Stella, each becomes at once unique and representative of late Victorian America. Together, they define the rural Western New York and Pennsylvania landscape in the Gay Nineties. Peopled with Norman and Stella's considerable acquaintance, the four settings assume a personal as well as a collective identity.

How Norman and Stella adapt to their respective environments reveals a great deal about them as individuals and about the expectations of their society. They are quintessential Victorians whose letters describe an awakening landscape. Emerging communities like Jamestown and Dubois offer opportunities beyond the family farm. Much like the landscape,

Norman and Stella are evolving, becoming adults. Their choices, however, are influenced by attitudes and values not only personal but societal. Duty and responsibility are not the same for Norman as for Stella. Norman seeks middle class success with a strict moral integrity. Stella's life is subject to the well-being of her family.

Certainly, their attitudes are shaped over the four years by experience. That they are physically separated for three of the four years presumes an experience that is largely separate. The emotional growth that accompanies their experience is also separate. What distinguishes their correspondence is that the courtship is not so much the defining as the common theme of that experience.

Norman and Stella speak with affecting guilelessness. Much of the impact of their letters derives from the honesty of their self-revelation. Their picture of Victorian society, though pretty, is often fraught with danger. Victorian society imposed strict restraints. Norman and Stella are, mercifully, unaware of their society's conditioning. From a twenty-first century perspective, the innocence of their honesty is sometimes charming, sometimes naive. Given human fragility, it is ultimately poignant.

The letters are written in script using primarily eight-inch by five-inch lined writing paper. Both Norman and Stella opened their letters with a letter opener and refolded them into their original envelopes. Most envelopes bear a two-cent George Washington profile stamp, some a two-cent "Landing of Columbus" stamp. The envelopes are addressed with the recipient's name, post office, and state, and sending and receiving postmarks appear on both sides. Stella had the habit of writing "ans" on the envelopes of letters to which she had already replied. A few of the letters have ink blots and crossed out words. Many have postscripts scrawled in the margins. Despite yellowing and minor fading, the letters are remarkably easy to read. Stella's penmanship is far more legible than Norman's. The letters have been transcribed using the original spelling and punctuation except for minor editing for the sake of clarity.

if nothing happens is organized into five chapters. The first four are bound by the three visits Norman and Stella shared in the three years between the Portland grape harvest and Norman's proposal. The fifth, corresponding to the final year of the courtship, includes the letters written after the proposal. Norman proposed to Stella at the Sparta farm in November 1895. Until their marriage the following November, he visited her frequently there. His visits that year provided emotional support after the deaths in her family. Their voluminous correspondence in 1896 is particularly revealing of the emotional growth each had experienced.

Norman and Stella's extensive circle of family and friends may initially be confusing. Notes are provided prior to the letters where needed to identify the various personalities and to present a historical context for the action. Many of the persons mentioned will become familiar through repeated reference. For easy identification a complete list of those mentioned in the letters *(dramatis personae)* is included in the front material of this book. Also included are several letters written by family or friends. These complementary letters are a delight to read. They both personalize their authors and shed further light upon the lives lived by Norman and Stella.

The reader is invited to pay attention to the efficiency of period mail delivery. The letters were delivered via railroad. Most were sent general delivery to the post office. Because Norman and Stella changed addresses often, their letters frequently had to be forwarded. This, of course, required notification to the post office of the recipient's new location. The importance of the post office is a subtle attribute of the Victorian life Norman and Stella hereby preserve.

Jennifer Riesmeyer Elvgren
December 14, 2000

Acknowledgments

My love of history began with the stories that my grandmothers, the late Marian Ingerson Riesmeyer and Grace Caccaro Taggart told me of their childhoods. I am grateful. Without the initial interest and encouragement of my uncle, the late Norman Harold Riesmeyer; my aunt, Barbara Riesmeyer Thomas; and family friend, Sue Mullen; this book would still be in cardboard boxes. I am thankful. I could not imagine a better first publishing experience than the one I had with Chautauqua Region Press. Paul Leone has loved Norman and Stella like his own family; taught me how to make a book; and along with his wife, Ann Servoss, made every trip I took to Jamestown feel like a homecoming. I am obliged. My ever loving friend and husband, Erik Cobden Elvgren, is my most ardent supporter, and my son, William Brigham Elvgren, is an endless source of joy. I am blessed.

During the research process, I dug through stacks of old books and files, talked for hours on the phone, sloshed through snow-covered cemeteries, and drove up and down many country roads. Along the way, I was shown many kindnesses and wish to warmly thank the Fenton Historical Society of Jamestown, New York; The Dubois Area Historical Society; Laura Polo and The Crawford County Historical Society; the First Baptist Church of Jamestown; the Dutch Treat; Christine Olson and the Spartansburg School; Mr. & Mrs. Ralph Davis; Mrs. Betty Murdock, Lyric Lyman Murdock's daughter-in-law; Mr. Clayton Ingerson, Floyd Ingerson's son; and Mr. & Mrs. George F. Long, who now own Pa Murdock's farm where Norman and Stella courted and married.

Dramatis Personae

Parentheses indicate subject's main residence during the courtship.

Chautauqua County

Ingerson, Susan Waterman, born Lime, New Hampshire, 1807; died Ellery Township, 1895.   Norman's grandmother. (Dewittville)

Ingerson, John Wilson, 1841-1910. Norman's father. (Dewittville)

Ingerson, Cornelia Haskin, 1843-1931. Norman's mother.

Ingerson, George H., 1866-1951. Norman's brother. (Fluvanna, Bemus Point)

Ingerson, Kate Reardon, born Centreville, South Dakota, 1872; died Jamestown, 1936. George's wife.   (Fluvanna, Bemus Point)

Ingerson, Mildred Ruth, 1891-1948. George and Kate's first child.

Ingerson, Howard George, born December 8, 1892. George and Kate's second child.

Ingerson, Mary Frances, born November 5, 1894. George and Kate's third child.

Ingerson, Floyd, 1882-1966. Norman's brother. (Dewittville)

Cheney, Mark, 1853-1907. Farmer, Ellery Township. Norman's brother-in-law.

Cheney, Frances Ingerson, 1865-1940. Norman's sister, Mark's wife.

Cheney, Minnie Kate, born September 1, 1890. Mark and Frances' first child.

Cheney, Ralph Ingerson, 1894-1949. Mark and Frances' second child.

Reardon, Nellie, Kate Ingerson's mother. (Mayville)

Reardon, Nellie, Kate Ingerson's sister. (Mayville)

Waterman, Asa L., 1848-1926. Norman's father's cousin. (Dewittville)

Waterman, Elizabeth Cobb, 1847-1912. Asa's wife.

Waterman, Eugene, 1871-1945. Asa and Elizabeth's second child, grape-picker.

Waterman, Leonora Briggs (Nora), 1873-1939. Eugene's wife, grape-picker.

Waterman, Martin Roselle (Martie), 1875-1934. Asa and Elizabeth's third child, grape-picker.

Waterman, Edith Cobb, 1873-1936. Martin's wife and cousin, grape-picker.

Waterman, Mattie, Asa and Elizabeth's fourth child, Fred Smith's wife, grape-picker.

Waterman, E.O., Asa's cousin.

Waterman, Norman O., 1849-1929. Asa's brother.

Cobb, "Aunt Addie", Edith's mother. (Dewittville)

Lewis, Rosetta, Norman and Stella's friend, grape-picker. (Dewittville)

Martin, J.P., owner, Southside Vineyard. (Brocton)

Francis, Mr. and Mrs. Smith T., owners, Maple Springs Hotel; Norman's uncle and aunt.

Gray, Silas (Uncle Siles), born Concord Township, Pennsylvania, 1846. Stella's mother's brother.

Hall, Oscar, grape-picker.

Goldstein, Gertie, grape-picker.

Dubois

Murdock, Irving Franklin (Irva), born Sparta Township, 1860. Stella's brother.

Murdock, Eliza Pierce, born Sparta Township, 1863. Irva's wife.

Murdock, Lulu Ethel, born Spartansburg, 1882. Irva and Eliza's first child.

Murdock, Durwood Belmont, born Britton Run, 1885. Irva and Eliza's second child.

Murdock, Mate Mildred, born Britton Run, 1887. Irva and Eliza's third child.

Allen, E.M., Irva's first business partner, American Artists Alliance.

Griesemer, J.M. (John), manager, American Artists Alliance.

Griesemer, P.E. (Phil), John's brother; second manager, American Artists Alliance.

Jack, employee, American Artists Alliance.

Curr/Kerr, Mr., employee, American Artists Alliance.

DeMotte, Miss, employee, American Artists Alliance.
Batts, Mr., grape-picker.

Sparta

Murdock, Franklin Warren (Pa), born Concord Township, Pennsylvania, 1838. Stella's father.
Murdock, Dorothy (Dot), Franklin's second wife, Stella's step-mother.
Murdock, William Ellsworth (Will), born Sparta, 1867. Stella's brother.
Murdock, Rose Weaver, 1872-1895. Will's wife.
Murdock, Lyric Lyman, 1891-1962. Will and Rose's first child.
Murdock, Clarice Rilla, born Sparta, 1882. Will and Rose's second child.
Murdock, Franklin Warren (Frankie), 1894-1896. Will and Rose's third child.
Murdock, Lella, Will's second wife.
Murdock, Alonzo (Uncle Lon), born Concord Township, 1851; died Sparta, 1927. Pa's brother.
Murdock, Jennie, 1857-1927. Uncle Lon's wife.
Haydon, Charlie, Stella's cousin, grape-picker.
Haydon, Clarence, Stella's cousin, grape-picker.
Frost, Evart, Spartansburg neighbor, Stella's friend.
Frost, Edna, Evart's wife, Stella's cousin.
Frost, Ida, Evart's sister.
Parker, Charlie, Edna Frost's brother, Stella's cousin, grape-picker.
Gray, Alonzo, (Uncle Lon Gray) Stella's mother's brother. (Titusville, Pennsylvania)
Gray, Lucinda, Alonzo's wife. (Titusville)
Gray, Dollie, Alonzo and Lucinda's daughter. Stella's childhood friend. (Titusville)
Dorne, Nora, Stella's friend, grape-picker.
Dorne, Ethie, Nora's sister, Stella's friend, grape-picker.
Harrington, Ida, 1871-1951. Stella's friend.

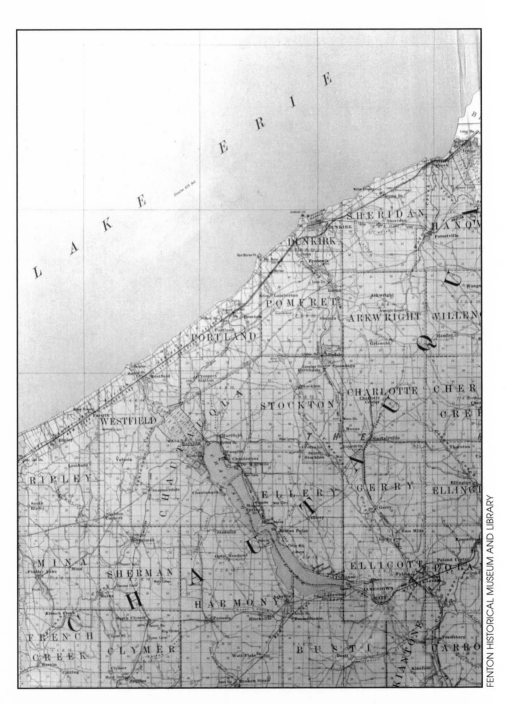

Bien, Joseph R., Atlas of the State of New York, Julius Bien & Co., New York, 1895.

Norman Wilson Ingerson, Ca. 1893   Stella May Murdock, Ca. 1893

I

friend Norman, friend Stella

Norman and Stella begin their correspondence enthusiastically following the five-week grape harvest. Their extended group of young friends, many of whom are mentioned in Norman's first letter, obviously enjoyed the seasonal work and the opportunity to spend time with each other. References to the harvest throughout the four-year correspondence are nostalgic. Norman wrote Stella immediately upon arriving "home" at his elder brother George's farm at Fluvanna, just above Jamestown, on the east side of Chautauqua Lake. The two had separated at Mayville only two days before.

Stella returned from the grape fields to her father's farm near Spartansburg, Pennsylvania, five miles south of Corry. She remained in Sparta only two days, then accompanied her "sister" (sister-in-law) Eliza Pierce Murdock to Dubois, Clearfield County, one-hundred-twenty miles east. Her elder brother Irving "Irva" had opened a portrait and framing studio in Dubois earlier in the year. Norman's letter reached her there.

It is easy to imagine Norman's disappointment, subtly stated, ("I was some surprized") on discovering in Stella's answer that she was so much farther out of reach. Nevertheless, the more difficult rail trip didn't stop him from carrying through on his plan to visit her during the Christmas holiday. Responsibilities of school and work prevented frequent visits over the next three years necessitating a long distance courtship. Returning to Jamestown in the new year, Norman confessed his feelings unabashedly.

Norman and Stella traveled together from Brocton, shipping center for the wine country, to Mayville at the head of Chautauqua Lake on the Western New York and Pennsylvania Railroad. Stella continued on the same line to Spartansburg while Norman, after seeing to a transfer of luggage, took the Chautauqua Lake Railway along the east side of the lake to Fluvanna. Kate Reardon Ingerson is George's wife and Norman's sister-in-law, who is eight months pregnant. Charlie Hayden and brother Clarence (letter Nov. 27, 1892) are Stella's cousins and her chaperones in the grape country.

Fluvanna, N.Y.
Nov 7 - 92
Monday morn
Dear friend Stella
I will now take the pleasure of writing to let you know that I
arrrived at home safely Sat night at half past six. I did not come
on the morning train as intended when we parted at Mayville,
Mrs Goldstien's and Rosetta Lewis's trunks did not come on the
train we did from Brocton so I staid till night at Mayville and had
them rechecked when the next train came. Kate came up to her
mother's Nellie Reardon's home at Mayville while I was there sat
aft so when I got home I found no one but George here We were
alone all day yesterday and you can't imagine how lonesome it
seemed after having been in a crowd for five weeks. How I wish
that you could have staid with us for a few days Stella, then the
time would have seemed much shorter; to me at least. I attended
church at Fluvanna yesterday Robt Jones the evangelist from
Jamestown is holding meetings there at present. I tell you Stella
no one but our dear Saviour and myself knows half what I owe
to this man and as I look back over my past life I shudder to
think where I stood when I first met Rob Jones. God bless him
and my earnest prayer is that the good work may still go on.
Yesterday was a lovely day here with us it seemed so good to
have the sun shine again after a week of such rainy weather I
wondered if it was just as pleasant at Sparta, but this morning it
is raining a little. when you write let me know how Nora's and
Ethie's trunk stood the journey give my respects to Charlie and
all of my fun friends at your place. I think I shall go to
Jamestown to day with George. I do not know where I shall go to
school this winter yet but have some thoughts of going to the
business college at Jamestown. I shall wait a while to find out
where Martie is going would like if possible to be with him this
winter it would be much pleasanter by the way that reminds me
that I must mail this letter and write one to him I shall count the
weeks and days till Christmas when if nothing happens I shall
come to visit you at your home write soon Stella and don't forget
to send me your picture as soon as possible
from your sincere friend
Norman Ingerson

Democrat Grover Cleveland is elected President. Dubois celebrates. Allusions to politics are generally superficial between Norman and Stella.

Du Bois. Pa.
Nov. 13th 92.
Sunday eve
Dear friend Norman: –
I now take pen in hand to answer your welcome letter which was rec'd in due time and contents read with interest. I arrrived home all safely only to stay untill Tuesday. My sister was out from Du Bois and was very anxious that I should go home with her, although I hated to leave home again so soon I concluded that I have better come now. We started at about half past eight and reached here at about two o'clock. We changed cars at Corry and Ridgeway. I am only about 120 miles from home. Du Bois is quite a large place having a population of between seven and eight thousand. Well I suppose if we were where Ethie and Nora is they would have the laugh on us over election, their trunk came through all right. There is going to be a parade here Monday night, wish you were going to be here. I may go home Christmas if my folks don't come out here. If I do I shall expect to see you and if I don't I would like very much to have you come out here. This has been a lovely day. I haven't been to church here yet. The electric light works are just across the road from us. I am writing in the store and there is so much talking going on that I can't think of much to write so please excuse this poor excuse of a letter hopeing to hear from you soon
I am your sincere friend,
Stella Murdock.
Du Bois, Pa.

Martie and Mattie Waterman, brother and sister, live near Dewittville. They are Norman's cousins. They are also related to Mr. E. O. Waterman, who in 1892 had an interest in the Southside Vineyard, Brocton. Both the Ingersons and the Reardons have family near Dewittville on the east side of the lake, including Norman's father John Wilson Ingerson. Jamestown Business College is easily accessible from Fluvanna via the Chautauqua Lake Railway. The depot at Jamestown's boat landing is only blocks from the college.

Fluvanna N.Y.
Thursday morn
Nov 17 1892.
Dear friend Stella

I rec'd your letter last night and was very glad to hear from you I
was some surprized to find you had gone to your brothers so
soon. but hope you will have a good time and enjoy yourself as
well as I think we all did in the grape country. I have not been
having as good a time since I left the town of Portland as while
there. I have seen some pretty lonesome days one week ago last
night George and Kate went to visit her uncle near Dewittville
and did not get back untill the next friday night and I was all
alone not a person came into the house in all that time. well in
those two days I lived over again the five weeks at Portland but
did not find much to regret for I believe I never enjoyed myself
before as I did then. I have had two letters from Martie since I left
there. the first one was written the next day after we left and
every word of it said homesick he said he did not know how
much he thought of the young people there untill they were all
gone. the last one I recd last night at the same time I did yours he
is coming home the last of this week and wants I should come up
and stay with him sat night which I shall if possible I was up to
Fathers last Saturday and did not come home untill Tuesday
night Mattie came down with me and expects to stay with us till
tomorrow. I said she came with me but think it would be nearer
correct to say I came with her for she drove her fathers horse and
expects to go home alone tomorrow I hope the above will not
look like flirting to you for such is not the case. E. O. Waterman is
not going to stay with J. P. Martin another season so Martie said
in his letter he expects to move his things from there and come
home this week. Eugene and Nora B. are going to be married
Wed. Nov 30. I have not recd an invitation yet but suppose I shall
how I wish you could be here then but I suppose that is impossible. If nothing happens I shall go to Jamestown to the Business
College this winter, shall board at home and go on the cars I
think I hope you will be at home xmas if you are I shall surely
come to see you. but if you stay at Du Bois I will come just the
same if possible. well I must close and go and help George

suppose he thinks it has been a long time since I begun writing this. please excuse all mistakes and write very soon and tell me more of your new home for I shall receive and read with interest everything you write I hope this will find you well and enjoying yourself. I must say goodbye for this time
I remain your sincere friend
Norman Ingerson

Stella's duties at the portrait studio include clerking at the front desk while she apprentices in portrait manufacture. Loneliness and the place of church are Victorian themes reiterated often in the Ingerson correspondence.

DuBois, Pa.
Sun. evening
Nov 27–'92
Dear friend Norman
as I did not attend church this evening, thought I would answer your welcome letter of the 17th inst. which was received in due season. I went to the M.E. church last Sunday night, the only time I have been since I came here. I think this a very lonesome place. There are not very many pretty buildings here, at least that I have seen, but there are some nice ones being built. I haven't commenced learning the art of enlarging pictures yet, but intend begining to-morrow so don't know yet whethor I shall like the work or not but think I shall I was not at all suprised to hear that Nora and Eugene were going to be married but hardly expected it quite so soon. Where is Miss Cobb now? Well, I suppose you are going or are about to go to school by this time. it seems rather strange to me to not be attending school. I cannot tell yet whether I will go home Christmas or not but presume I will not as I have been here so short a time and think my folks may come out here. Did you go to Martie's? Is Mattie going to school? that makes me think I aught to write to her I suppose she is as happy as ever. I saw Mr. Batts in town the day I came out here so I guess he arrived home all safely. I wonder how Clarence is getting along. Do you know whether he got work or not? I will bring my letter to a close for this time hopeing to hear from you soon and all

about the wedding.
I am your sincere friend.
Stella Murdock.

The first of the weddings between Norman and Stella's young friends. Eugene is Martie and Mattie Waterman's older brother. Norman intends to board in Jamestown rather than commute to Jamestown Business College. This letter marks the beginning of Norman's energetic and active life, which will be contrasted to Stella's increasing isolation.

Fluvanna N.Y.
Dec 4th 1892.
Sun morn
Dear friend Stella
I now take pen in hand to answer your very welcome letter of one week ago. I have so much news to tell I don't know where to begin but I think if we were together I could talk a great deal in a very short time. I went to the wedding of course had quite a good time good as expected to. Martie was there with his "B.B." there was snow enough so that nearly everybody came with sleighs They were married at 11 a.m. and immediately after dinner were driven to Dewittville where they took the cars for Buffalo. Their stay in that place was very short they came back the next day. They recieved a nice lot of presents among which were a full set of blue china, an extension table two lamps one doz. silver knives and forks and seven table cloths. etc etc, a number of us attended church services at Dentons schoolhouse that evening sermon by Elder Miller of Forestville I staid with Martie that night and drove home in the morning. have been helping George cut wood lately when at home which is not more than half of the time I went up to Marties when I wrote you I was going to and went over to Portland with Eugene and Martie after some of Eugene's goods it seemed very lonesome over there. there was nobody there but J. P. and Oscar Hall. I staid with Martie three days that time then he came home with me and staid one night so you see we have managed to be together most of the time. Miss Cobb came down here yesterday is going to

work for George this winter I heard that Clarence got work near Portland. don't know where he is now. well I guess I shall have to take another sheet of paper to finish this letter I intend to begin going to the Business College tomorrow shall board in Jamestown for a while I think because of a change of time on the railroad making it impossible for me to go on the cars. I hope you will like your new work it must be quite a change from grape picking. Mattie said she got a letter from Ethie a few days ago and is expecting one from you O yes I forgot to tell you that Eugene and Nora were married by Elder Stubbs of Portland there were about seventy present at the wedding. When we parted at Mayville one month ago it seemed as though Christmas would never come but now as it is only three weeks till then I think perhaps the time will pass somehow. when you find out where you will be Christmas dont fail to write in time for me to make calculations beforehand and I will surely come and see you if I will be welcome and something does not happen to make it impossible. by the way I haven't seen anything of that photograph you promised me please send it as soon as possible. I will bring this to a close hoping to hear from you very soon. I remain very sincerely your friend
Norman Ingerson

The options by rail to Dubois are to take the Erie line west to Corry and transfer to the Pennsylvania line, or to travel east from Jamestown through Salamanca to Bradford and there transfer. Irva's business thrives at his first holiday season. The first of more than twenty deaths mentioned in the letters.

Sunday,
Dec. 11, 1892.
Dear Friend:
It is with pleasure I sit down this afternoon to answer your welcome letter which arrived Wednesday and to inform you that I am not going home for the holidays therefore will expect to see you out here about a week from Saturday. If you come by the way of Corry you can not get through unless you leave there on the 9 o'clock train I think that is the nearest way that you can come, but if you start from Jamestown please let me know as you

would come in at a different depot. Well as I commenced this letter before church and did not finish it will now proceed to write a few more lines, went to the Presbyterian church and heard a lovely sermon the church is a new one but is not quite finished it is going to be very nice. I received a letter from Rosetta the other day she said she was at school and saw Nora and Eugene go by to the depot so suppose she was not at the wedding. I have met some of the young folks since I came here think I am going to like living here first rate as I get better accquainted. Irva (my brother) is very busy now making holiday deliveries. Letha Miller Ethie & Nora's cousin who we was talking about as being sick so long died recently I can hardly make it seem possible, she was such a lively girl when well. There has been no sleighing here yet to speak of. I guess I will close for this time as I think of nothing more to write hopeing to hear from you soon I am as ever your friend
Stella Murdock.
DuBois, Clearfield County. Penna.

Norman is visiting George in Fluvanna. He has taken up the bookkeeping course at Jamestown Business College, which continues alive and well today. Howard Ingerson, George and Kate's second child, is born.

Fluvanna N.Y.
Dec 1892
Dear Freind Stella
 I received your welcome letter last thursday and it is with pleasure I sit down to answer it and tell you that I intend to come down to your place Sat. next the 24th Inst. I shall start from Jamestown at twenty five minutes past eight and come by the way of Bradford. I cannot tell what time I shall reach your place but think it will not be later than noon if I make close connections at Bradford. George is the happiest fellow I know of he has got a boy one week old last Thursday. I was up and stayed with Father last night and today went up to Martin Waterman's. We went to Sunday School at the school house near there. Mattie was writing to you when I left there about five this afternoon. I have been to

school two weeks and like it very well indeed. It seems rather queer to be going to school with nothing to do nights and mornings after being at work all summer. Well I will say good night for this time hoping to see you ere another week goes by.
I am as ever your sincere friend
Norman W. Ingerson.

The correspondents understand that a letter must be answered before either party will write again. Victorian etiquette requires, however, that a visitor inform the visited of his safe return. Letters following visits are among the most revealing. Norman and Stella will not see each other again for eight months.

Jamestown, N.Y.
Jan. 2nd 1893
Dear Stella
You will excuse me for writing this on business letter paper for I have no other here. I am writing at my desk in school I arrived home all safely at about half past five and have been over to my boarding place to supper but I felt so lonesome thought I would come up here where it is quiet and write to you. It was a long lonesome ride and I was glad when it came to an end. had to wait in Bradford about an hour. My boarding mistress thinks George will be down tomorrow and if he comes I think I shall go home with him for a day or so. I don't know whether you can read this or not I feel so tired and nervous I cannot write decent. I think I realize tonight more than ever before how much you are to me now that we are so far seperated I feel that I would give most anything to be with you as I was last night but as that is impossible I shall have to make the best of it and go to work at my studies as soon as possible well I can't think of much to write so I will close hoping this will find you well and happy.
I am your loving friend
Norman W. Ingerson
(57) fifty seven Marvin Street
Jamestown N.Y.

Third Street, Jamestown, Ca. 1895. Jamestown Business College then occupied rooms in the Gokey Building across Cherry Street from the Presbyterian Church. The trolley in the foreground is turning south on Main.

letter received contents noted

*In frequent correspondence before they next meet in early
September, Norman and Stella begin to define themselves. They
are both twenty-years-old, not quite adult. Their plans for the
future are uncertain and their expressions of affection tentative
("Pshaw what a goose I am"). Their romance has ripened to the
point, however, that Stella's grape-picking friends tease her over
it.*

*Norman successfully completes the Commercial Course at
Jamestown Business College, then accepts temporary employment
offered by family and friends. Stella settles in rather ambivalently
to life at Dubois. Her days are filled with studio and household
work, church, and the occasional social engagement. Irva is frequently away on business. He is thirty-two-years-old, the father
of three children, and upwardly mobile. Stella's presence in his
household eases the child care burden for Eliza. Expectation and
opportunity related to gender emerge subtly in these letters.
Norman's aggressive pursuit of career will continue to contrast
with Stella's passive attitude.*

*The pace of late Victorian life in small town America is reflect-
ed. Entertainments include sleighing in winter, corn popping,
candy pulls, parades and picnics, frequent visitations, and letter
writing. Chautauqua Lake features a summer resort season. The
Columbia Exposition opens in Chicago. Stella's visit to
Spartansburg in the fall enables Norman to see her again.*

Sparta

Jan. 4 1893

My much beloved Daughter Stella

I hope you won't blame me for not writing sooner. I was agoing
to try and write but Willey came down and I was fealing so poorly he staid and helped me about my choars he wants to say to
Irvy that he will take the hous for one year as Irvy offerd and
Willey pay the taxes he thought it quite a rent at first but after
thinking it all over concluded it was as cheap as he could aford it
I sopose Irvy got back that day from rigway all right dident he,
how very kind it was in him to go with me, I think all of you was
great as good to me as could be tel Mr Grismer my wife thought
the picture very nice I sopose Norman went home the next day
you dident ask me what I thought of him, my head feals so bad I
cant hardly write atall so good by for this time

from your afecenate father

F.W. Murdock

*Norman's boarding house at 57 Marvin Street, (today Washington Street near
the corner of Eighth), is a short distance from Jamestown Business College and
the Chautauqua Lake Railway depot at the boat landing. "Pa," Franklin
Warren Murdock, whose ill health is a constant concern to Stella, spends
Christmas in Dubois. Norman meets him for the first time at Irva's house.
Lulu Murdock is the eldest of Irva and Eliza's three children.*

Jan 8th 93.

Sunday evening

Dear Friend Norman: –

Was very glad to hear that you arrived home all safely and hope
that your visit was a pleasant one. Irva said he intended to have
seen you again before you went away. I received a letter from Pa
the other day, he is not well yet but was feeling better than he did
while here. Lulu has been sick but I guess will be able to go to
school again to-morrow. Well this week has seemed somewhat
longer than last week did. I did not go up to the store to work the
day you went away but helped Eliza wash. How did the lunch

you took with you stand the journey? was sorry you didn't have more. The church bells are ringing but guess I wont go as Eliza does not want to go with me. I will close for this time excuse this short letter and write soon.

Good night. from

Your friend, Stella Murdock.

DuBois, Pa.

Norman responds immediately from his boarding house. His elder sister Frances is married to Mark Cheney, whose family owns substantial property a short distance above Fluvanna. Contagious disease is always a threat to Victorian families. A Christmas "Tree" is a public holiday gathering featuring a decorated tree. Edith Cobb is Martie and Mattie Waterman's cousin.

Jan. 10th

Tuesday Evening

My Dear freind Stella

Received your welcome letter this afternoon and was very glad to hear from you. This has been a very cold bleak day mercury stood at 1 below 0 this morning and only three degrees above at one P.M. and it snows and blows a perfect gale all the time. I did not go home last week as I thought I would when writing you before. Kate came for me Friday Afternoon though, and it seemed quite good to get home after having been away nearly three weeks. Miss Cobb was there then but went away Saturday and they have a young girl working there now by the name of Thompson. was at my sisters last Saturday evening. Did not go anywhere to church Sunday. I am glad to hear your Father is better than when at Du Bois. you didn't say anything about how you are getting along with your art are you still making eyes? There is a great deal of diptheria about Fluvanna now one family had five deaths within two weeks 4 children and their mother. We all are hoping that so much cold weather will stop its spreading. I received a letter from Martie last friday. he said he did not go anywhere Christmas not even to a Tree because it was so stormy I suppose. I will quote one little extract from his letter see if you dont think it sounds just as you would expect to hear him talk if you saw him he said "did you have a good time while in Du Bois I'll Bet Stella did if you didn't." I can only say I hope you had as pleasant a time as I did as it is getting late I will bring this to a close sending my love to all.

I remain as ever

Your loving freind

Norman.

Jan. 15-1893.

Dear friend:

With pleasure I will endeavor to answer your welcome letter which found me well and hope this will reach you the same. Eliza has not been feeling well for nearly a week, although she is up around. Irva tried to get her to go and see the doctor but as she would not, he had him come to the house, yesterday, she is some better to day. I have been making ears since you went away, and have done sound sketching besides. Have you recovered from your cold yet? There seems to be a good deal of sickness now. Mrs. Gorden's little boy is sick, the doctor does not seem to know what is the matter of him, it may be the scarlet fever as there are several cases of it in town. I haven't been to church to day as I did not care to go alone in fact I have not been since you was here. Don't you think I am getting rather negligent about going to church? Protracted meetings are being held here now. I think I shall attend them some if I can coax Eliza to go when she gets well enough. Irva has been popping corn wish you were here to eat some. Where is Miss Cobb now? It seems that Martie is still in the habit of Betting. Irva's store looks quite different since you were here as he has it newly carpeted and a lovely book-case and writing desk combined in it. Will say, Good bye for this time, write soon from your friend.

Stella Murdock.

Written from George's farm. Sunday is visiting day, and Kate and George have gone to Mayville. Norman's father and ten-year-old brother, Floyd, have come down to Fluvanna from Dewittville. Norman's father and mother are estranged. That Norman addresses Edith Cobb formally as "Miss" and Eliza as "Mrs. Murdock" implies a brief acquaintance.

Fluvanna N.Y.
Jan 22–
Dear Stella:–
I received your very welcome letter last Wednesday, but was so busy that I could not answer it until to day so I suppose I will not receive an answer this week. Was sorry to hear that Mrs. Murdock was not well. Tell her I send her my sympathy if it will help her any. I have been working quite hard at my studies for the last week or so. Tried 2 examinations last week and if I passed will be advanced to the next higher room tomorrow. There are a course of Revival meetings being held at the Methodist Church I have only been two nights and that is all I have been to church since coming home from Pa. Suppose I ought to go more but have been very busy. I wish it was possible for me to be with you once a week at least perhaps we would both attend church more regularly. George and Kate are at Mayville to day visiting Kates mother I think miss Cobb is at Mayville also. Pa and Floyd are here to day. I was at my sisters last Sunday and we had a candy pull it made me think of a certain night last fall wish we could all be together again as we were then for a little while. I received a letter from Martie last Thursday They are all well up there he said. he did not write very much news but I like to get letters from my freinds whether there is much news in them or not. I have not been up there since before Christmas but intend to go the first Sat. that I can get George to stay at home. It is excellent sleighing here I wish you would come up this way we would improve it some I'll Bet. Kate said when I first came home that she wished you could come up and stay a week so I think perhaps you would be welcomed by all. Well I stopped writing this morning rather abruptly but will now try and finish this. It is now 8 o'clock in the evening. I went about two miles up the lake to take the hired-girl home and took dinner at my sister's. Georges folks have got home and the people at Mayville are all well. Do you have lots of snow and good sleighing in Du Bois? I hope you may have lots of sleighrides and

a good time. Well I guess I have written all the news I can think of this time so I will close this and write to Martin.
Hopeing to hear from you soon.
Good night,
Your loving freind,
Norman Ingerson

Jan. 24 1893:
Dear Friend
Your letter received to-day and read with pleasure. Eliza and Lulu have gone to the Opera House where there is a Ball to-night to watch them dance a while, and Derwood & Mate have gone to bed therefore, I am nearly alone and thought I would write a few lines to you. Eliza is feeling some better but is far from being well and Irva has gone to Ridgeway he is away from home nearly all the time. I hope you will pass in your examinations if you dislike them as I used to, I think I know how to sympathise with you. I went to M.E. Church and Sunday school Sunday forenoon and in the evening to Presbyterian Church enjoyed both very much. The snow is not very deep here and the sleighing is fine. I haven't had the first sleigh ride think I would enjoy a few if I were at home. Do you still board where you did and how does those red-headed girls get along? I received the calendar allright and thought it a pretty one. Norman I will bring my letter to a close for this time as it is getting late and news are rather scarce with me at least. Eliza has not returned yet wouldn't wonder but what she has run accross some pretty fellow. hoping to hear from you soon.
Your friend Good night, Stella Murdock.

Jamestown N.Y.

Jan 26

Dear friend Stella,

I was very pleasantly Surprized on going to dinner to day to find your letter waiting for me. Yes! I am still boarding at the same place do not like it very well either. Those Red-headed girls are very annoying sometimes. I passed my examinations allright and am now in the Practical Department The first thing I did on coming into this Dep. was to make out a lease for an imaginary store Then they gave me $500 in College Currency. Then we students do actual business with one another and keep our own book accounts I think it will be quite interesting and beneficial also. This has been a lovely day and quite warm for this season. Have you heard from your Father lately and is he feeling better than he did? It is about the same as usual tonight I can't think of very much to write but can think of plenty I could tell you if I could see you so will say good night Stella, for this time

Your loving freind

Norman

P.S.-Write soon

Ethie and Nora Dorne are sisters and Stella's friends from Sparta. E. M. Allen is Irva's first business partner. J.M. (John) Griesemer serves as the store manager. Miss Demotte and Mr. Curr, apparently, are staff workers.

Du Bois, Pa.,
Feb. 3d. 1893
Dear Friend Norman.
Received your welcome letter Saturday and will now take pen in hand to answer it. I am writing at the store therefore excuse this paper. I have been very busy this week, trying to sketch an old man to-day. I do not get along very fast at least it does not seem to me that I do. I recieved a letter from Ethie & Nora to-day which was very interesting. Nora said to give you her best respects. one of them wanted to know if I was having as good a time as we had while at Portland Well, I should say no, not exactly. Mr. Allen came home with Irva Friday and they went to Bradford Monday. Irva expects to be gone two weeks this time. he got some medicine to cure the tobacco habit but it made him so sick that he did not take it all. The last I heard from home Pa was feeling better. Eliza is still feeling very poorly she went to see a different doctor last evening so I am now in hopes that she will feel better soon. It has been very rainy, lonesome weather here for the last few days. It is not raining to-day but the wind is blowing very hard. Have you seen Martie since you were here? I received a letter from Mattie a short time ago. Mr. Greisemer, Miss DeMotte and another person are talking about churches. I am very glad that I do not believe as they seem to concerning religion. I attend Sunday school quite regularly of late, at the M.E. Church. My teacher's name is Mr. Chestnut. Mr. Curr told me to send you his love. I will close for this time hopeing to hear from you soon. I am as ever,
Your sincere friend,
Stella Murdock.

Mention of Nellie Waterman indicates that Norman and Stella had visited George during the grape harvest. Lakewood is a few stops west of the depot at Jamestown's boat landing.

Jamestown,
Feb 7, 1893
Seven P.M. at my Boarding place
My dear friend Stella, –
How do you do tonight I am well and hope this will find you the same I recieved your very welcome letter yesterday. We have been having some very rainy weather lately but it is quite cold tonight. I was up to Martie's one week ago last Sunday and had a very pleasant time. it stormed while I was there and the snow being very deep made it nearly impossible for a horse to travel on the roads consequently I was obliged to stay till Monday Morn and did not get to school untill afternoon. Marties cousin, Nellie Waterman was there visiting. It was she that was at Eugene's the Sunday that We were at my brothers. perhaps you remember her anyway. Last Friday afternoon I went to Lakewood on the Street-Cars and walked across the Lake to Georges. The Lake is about 1 1/2 miles wide at that place and it was a very cold walk I can tell you. George's folks were gone away and did not get home untill Sunday afternoon Last Sunday was a very nice day and the sleighing was the best I ever saw. I went and took the hired girl home and that was all the sleigh ride I had. I sincerely wished that it had been with you, perhaps we would have driven a little "further." Katie has named the baby "Howard George." how do you like that for a name. How do you get along sketching that old man. Tell Mr. Greisemer (if you want to) that I think you would do better sketching some good-looking young fellow. I am getting along first-rate with my studies and think that with good luck I may get through by the first part of May. It rained all day yesterday and today the streets are ice all over. people do not use the sidewalks very much but walk in the middle of the streets or anywhere that there is a chance of stand-ing up. I do not go to church very much of late not as much as I would like to at least. Tell Mr. Curr I was glad to know he remembers me; and that I retain a chair by memory's fireside for him. I hope you will not wait as long before answering this as you did the last.
goodnight
your loving friend
Norman Ingerson

A stroll through Dubois. The town was nearly destroyed by fire in 1888. A lumber and coal center, it boasts in 1892 a telephone toll station, electric lights for 750 residents, and gas heating. A trolley system and hospital are under construction, and the first high school class is about to graduate.

Feb 14 1893.
Dear friend Norman
I now embrace a few spare moments in answer to your letter which I was very glad to receive and also to learn that you are getting along so nicely with your studies. It is raining to-night which puts me in mind of the night we were at Mr. Pecks. I wonder where Will (the wall flower) is by this time and also the Star of the evening. Irva has been out to Spartansburg on a short visit. I sometimes wish I was there too but then Such is life you know. There is but little snow here now, the streets have been a perfect glare of ice and several have been hurt very badly by falling or coasting. Curr fell and cut his knee and had to have several stitches taken in it but it is now getting better so that he can walk on it without limping much. We (Eliza and I) went to a play last Friday night called The Boy Tramp. I did not like it very well but others seemed to think it was splendid. Eliza & I took quite a walk Sunday viewing the town. Du Bois looks like quite a place when you are on the hill looking down. Irva went to Punxsutawney to day it seems good not to see him smoking any more. There is another boiler being put in the electric lighthouse so I suppose we will have more music than ever after while. Well I will close for this time write soon
from your friend
Stella Murdock.

Fluvanna, N.Y.,
Feb. 19, 1893
Dear Freind, –
I received your very welcome letter last Friday and was glad to
hear that Irva has stopped smoking and hope he will stick to it.
George has gone to take the hired girl home and Kate and I are
here alone with the children. The baby is getting so he is quite
cute and Mildred is the worst little mischief I ever saw. We have
been having very lonesome rainy weather lately but yesterday
and today have been cold and stormy. How are you getting along
with picture making? I was at school yesterday and did some
copying I drove down, got there about noon and came back in
time to help do the chores at night The sleighing continues good
in spite of the rain the road being coated with ice all over. I began
last week taking lessons on a Type-writer with an hours practise
every day, I think I shall like it first rate when I get a little used
to it. I was at the Presbyterian church and heard a fine sermon
Wednesday Eve. about all that I go to church lately is one night
in the middle of a week. One week ago to day I was up to my
Aunts near Dewittville and attended church there. Twas one of
the nicest winter days I ever saw. We have a Literary and
Debating society at the College that meets every Thursday Eve. It
is quite interesting we have recitations songs etc. and sometimes
a debate Last week the question for debate was "Resolved that
Capital Punishment should be abolished" The Negative side won
by a unanaimous vote of the Judges.
Sunday Evening
Well Stella I will try and finish this letter which I began this
morning This is a very stormy night. I have just been and got
Miss Thompson (The hired girl) and stopped at my sisters a little
while I don't think I was ever out in a worse storm than to night.
George has been popping corn and it is very nice. I wish you was
here to eat some with me, (not with the rest of course.) Well I
must say good night for this time write soon
from your loving freind
Norman Ingerson

J.P.Martin of Southside Vineyard has taken a bride. He had been known among his employees as a confirmed bachelor, a man who over-imbibed and spat on the carpet. Irva's family occupies a two- unit flat. The neighbors are preparing to move.

Mar. 5 -'93.
Sunday eve.
Norman Ingerson.
Jamestown, N.Y.
Dear friend Norman

I will now answer your letter of the 19 ult which was received in due time and contents read with pleasure. How are you enjoying yourself this cold weather? It has been snowing here to-day. Mrs. Watterson an accquiantance of Eliza's from Titusville is here visiting came Thursday and I guess will go home Tuesday wouldn't care if I was going as far as Spartansburg with her. Heard from home yesterday. Pa has been very sick again I don't know as he has been as sick as the word "very" would indicate in the above, but he has been a good deal as he was while here. It makes me wish that I was with him when I hear that he is not well. Norman you need not be any surprised to read almost anything in this letter for Mrs. Watterson is talking to me so much of the time, I hardly know what I am writing. Irva has been popping corn. Don't you wish you was here to eat some? (it is too salty.) Well such nonsense don't let anyone read this letter, I heard that Mr. Martin and Satina Tinesta Beatrice Thompson were married. I was quite surprised. I am still working at sketching Mr. Yoders people intend moving soon we hate to have them move they are such good neighbors. Well I will bring this appology of a letter to a close hoping to hear from you soon.
I am your friend
Stella

*Irva offered Norman a position "travelling" during Norman's Christmas visit
(letter, May 14, 1893). Norman's letter seeking a bookkeeping position at the
studio is missing.*

DuBois, Pa.,
March 9 – 1893
At the store.
Dear friend Norman
As your letter is included with some other writing that Irva
wished me to do I will now proceed to answer it. He does not
need any one to keep books for him as he has not enough work
of that kind to keep any one busy. Mr. Griesemer has the care of
what little work there is of that kind. I hope you will be success-
ful in getting a good position. This seems quite like a Spring
morning. Will bring this to a close hoping to hear from you soon.
Your friend
Stella Murdock.
Du Bois, Pa.

*Maple Springs is a small lakeside community between Fluvanna and
Dewittville and across the lake from Chautauqua Institution. Norman's aunt
and uncle, Mr. and Mrs. Smith T. Francis, operate the Maple Springs hotel,
one of many family owned boarding houses that encircled Chautauqua Lake at
the end of the century.*

Fluvanna N.Y.,
Mar 12, -93
Sunday afternoon
Dear freind Stella.
I received your welcome letter last Tuesday, and was glad to
know you was well; but sorry to hear you father's health is so
poor. It seems as though the farm is too hard a place for a person
with such poor health as he has. I was not much surprised to
hear that Irva did not want anybody to work for him, but
thought it would do no harm to make sure. We have been having
some very nice warm weather here for the last week though it is

snowing today. My Aunt, Mrs. Francis of Maple Springs, a small summer resort near opposite Chautauqua, was here yesterday and I went home with her and stayed last night. had a very pleasant visit and came home at noon on the train.

I received a letter from Martin W., the same day as yours he says his school is out now and he expects to go farming again. I did not think he was rejoicing a great deal over the fact. I have not been up there but once since I was at DuBois. Would like to go first rate, but would much prefer to Come to see you, Stella! it is not possible for me to tell on paper how I want to see you, but I suppose all is for the best and I hope I may be able to make you a visit soon after I finish my school. Three evenings last week I attended Evangelistic services at the Baptist Church of Jamestown and heard some very fine sermons by Dr. Kennard of Chicago. I had a chance to hire out to My Aunt of whom I have just spoken to work at her Boarding House but thought it hardly right to spend time and money for an education and then go to work in a boarding house if I can find anything better. Well I will close this and say goodbye for this time, hoping to hear from you very soon, I remain as ever.

Your loving friend
Norman

A typical Victorian traveling entertainment is described. Stella's description sounds straight from the tour guide.

Sunday,
March 26 -'93
Dear friend: –
How do you do to day, I am well and hope you are the same. Received a letter from home yesterday Pa is sick yet and not able to work he has a young man to do chores. I am quite worried about him. would like to go home first rate but don't intend to take the time until July or August unless he gets worse or I get too homesick before that time. I did not go to church this morn- ing. I went last evening to see a family that was found in a cave

in Arizona and are on exibition here, they are supposed to have been a race inhabiting this continent before the Indians. They show every appearance of having been an intelligent, civilized people as they were wrapped in heavy coarse cloth, which proves that they understood the process of weaving. They have high foreheads, small bones and fine hair, they are not petrified but the flesh seems to be dried caused by the state of the atmosphere in the cave where they were found. There are three men a woman and child, it is thought that the child (a little girl) was buried alive because there was a string around it which ties its hands and its head is turned as though trying to bite the string and its hands are in a Shape that shows that is was in terrible agony they said it was found beside the woman and it is supposed that it was their custom to bury a child alive with its mother. Have you succeeded in getting a position at book keeping yet. I think as you say I would hate to work in a boarding house (if I were you) after receiving an education that would permit me to work at something better. Mrs Snyder's (the lady now living in the other part of this house) mother is not expected to live, and Eliza and Irva have been down to see her. The danceing class gave a ball in the room under the copying house awhile ago. Miss DeMott tried to get me to go but as I do not dance I did not Eliza & Irva went and stayed a little while. Irva is going away (he says) to be gone four weeks but I hardly think he will be gone that long, he took dinner the other day at my uncle's in Mt Jewett. Well as supper is ready I will close for this time if you can't read this just lay off a day or else employ some good lawyer to read it to you. Good by hoping to hear from you soon
I am as ever your friend
Stella.

Norman's father lives with his mother, Norman's grandmother, Susan Waterman Ingerson, near Dewittville.

At home,
April 1, – 93
Saturday Evening
Dear Freind, –
how do you do to-night! I am well and hope this will find you the same. Was very sorry to hear that your fathers health is so poor. I was up to Martin Watermans two weeks ago and had a very good visit. Mattie was at Mayville visiting her cousin Nellie Reardon, Martin and I attended church and Sunday School at the school-house near there and heard a very good sermon. We are having quite warm weather here lately and it seems quite good after such a long winter. How are you getting along with Photo-Copying, making good progress, I hope. I think I am getting along as well as could be expected with my school. have been in the Office Department about one week and like it first rate. I almost dread to think of the time when I shall be through school and yet am anxious to be earning something. I have not yet found any employment but trust I will, by the time my schooling is finished, which will probably be nearly the 1st of June. Are Mrs. Murdock and the children all well. How I would like to see them tonight! (not you of course). George's baby is getting so he is quite cute and the little girl is about the worst mischeif I ever saw. I did not attend church any this week in fact I have not been to church since I was at M.R.W.s two weeks ago. Well I will say "good night!" and perhaps I may write more tomorrow
Norman.
Sunday evening.
I will try and finish this poor excuse of a letter I have been today up to my Grandmother's where Father lives. It was a long muddy ride, my sister Mrs. Cheney went with me. We had all the warm sugar we could eat. have you had any new maple sugar? I wish you could have been there today it was very nice I am talk-ing of driving to school from home after this week, so when you write please direct in care of "Jamestown Business College" and I will get letters there anyway all right. I wish I could tell you to

night all that is in my thoughts. How many times I have thought of all the pleasure I had during my visit with you this winter and wonder when I can come again But Pshaw what a goose I am anyway! Well I can't help it anyhow I must say what I think sometimes. I hope you will have good success in reading this I hardly think I could after it gets cold well I must say goodby for this time
write soon
I am as ever your loving freind
Norman

April 20, 1893,
Dear friend
Received your very welcome letter sometime ago but as I have been sick have neglected answering it. I am feeling much better now and think I will be able to be out again within a week or so I had the Scarlitena or first stage of scarlet fever. Matie and Lulu have also been sick with it so you see we have had quite a sick time of it here. Irva & Eliza have gone to a social at the Opera House given by The Ladies of the Relief Corps. Irva came home Monday after being gone about 3 weeks It is raining hard to-night this is a terrible looking place now where we live, nothing much but mud all around us. we would like to move but empty houses are so very scarce don't know as we can. I suppose you have not very many more weeks of school and aren't you glad. I have not been to church since Easter morning. Did you read Dr. Tallmages easter sermon. I thought it grand. Well the people of the house have returned and say they did not go to the social. The last I heard from home Pa was feeling some better he said he had lost 40 lbs. in weight. I think he must look rather slim he sent us some maple syrup and we intend having some warm sugar some day. Well Norman it is the same old story nothing much to write so I will close for this time hoping this will find you and your people all well.
I am as ever your friend Stella.
P.S. Do not wait as long as I did before answering.
Goodby

Norman's answer to the previous letter is missing. He is hoping for a position on a Chautauqua Lake steamboat. The Chautauqua Assembly opens its twentieth season in July. Chautauqua Institution remains a major cultural attraction on Chautauqua Lake. North Clarendon, just south of Warren, is an easy trip by rail to Spartansburg, which accounts for Stella's irritation with Irva for not having visited their ailing father.

Sunday May, 7, 1893.
Dear friend Norman
With pleasure I will now seat myself to answer your kind & welcome letter of the 30th ult which was duly received. I have been down to Mrs. Berringer's this afternoon (the family just below us) which is the fartherest I have been away from the house for over three weeks and I can assure you it has seemed like a long time to be shut up in the house but think unless I get worse again will be able to go to work within another week. I think the position you have in view a good one and hope you will be successful in getting it. Are you going to have commencement exercises I think from the picture of the J.B.C. it must be a very nice building. When does the assembly convene the first of July does it not?
-Tuesday-
Well I commenced this letter Sun. and we had callers and I did not finish it. We are having lovely weather now and it seems good after so much rain. Irva returned home again to-day has been to Bradford & North Clarendon was not so very far from Sparta when at N.C. and I am just provocked at him for not going home. Mr. Griesemer's brother in Buffalo has been out visiting him, he is also an artist I am not progressing very fast lately at photo copying. Eliza says to tell you she is glad to hear of your success in school. I will close for this time.
hoping to hear from you soon, from your friend
Miss Stella Murdock
DuBois, Pa.

Visiting day. Maple Springs is ten short stops from Fluvanna on the Chautauqua Lake Railway.

Fluvanna, N.Y.
5-14
Dear friend Stella,
I received your very welcome letter last Wednesday and was sorry to know that you have been confined to the house so long I hope that this will find you much better. I am at my sisters to day Georges people are away to Kate's brothers visiting so I came up here and think I shall go up to Maple Springs this afternoon at 3 o'clock on the train visiting so don't be surprised if this is post marked "M.S." I am more than glad to be able to say I finished the Commercial course at the J.B.C. last Friday and received my Diploma although it is a little hard to write that I have not yet found a Position. I have not yet found out about my Steamboat work but hardly think I shall get it. don't think from the above that I am discouraged for I will not get discouraged over such small things. Professor H.E. Parker wants me to stay and take the Shorthand and Type writing course. would like to ever so much but scarcely think it will be possible. Perhaps after a few months if I get something to do so to earn a little I may try to go. I do not know when the Assembly begins but about the first of July I presume don't you think you might come out sometime this summer and make your headquarters at our house and go to Chautauqua for a week or so I believe you might if you only think so. O Yes! I was going to have you ask Irva if the offer he made me last winter of travelling for him was still standing. If so and I find nothing better I might come down and see what I could do for him. You can't imagine how much I would like to come down to your place anyway. My sisters people have company and I can't half write so I will say goodbye for this time write soon
from your
Loving freind
Norman.
P.S. Address me at Fluvanna Chaut, N.Y. until I am more sure where I shall be.
N.W.I.

Sunday
May 28th '93
Dear friend Norman
I will now seat my self this afternoon to answer yours of the 14th which I received a week ago yesterday. I asked Irva about your canvassing for him and he said to tell you that he has a full crew of agents now and all he wants, but that he will sell you some work and you can pay for it when you get the money out of it instead of your working for him and he giving you a percentage, if you have any territory out that way you think you could canvass but, I hope you may find something else to do for I don't think you would like the picture business may be I am wrong though. Irva has been gone nearly six weeks this trip, is away from home a great deal of the time. One of his agents Mr. Goss. came home with him last evening to stay over Sunday Mr. Griesemer took dinner with us to day. How are you enjoying so much rainy weather? Rather discouraging to farmers I think. There was a fire here several nights ago which occured at about 1 o'clock in the morning maybe we did not get out of bed quick when that awful shrill fire whistle blowed it was a mill that burnt. Well it seems good to be able to be out of doors again I went to a circus last Monday (Walter Mains) I believe I have heard you say you did not believe in going to shows haven't I? Oh well, I do. I haven't heard from Ethie & Nora for a long time guess they have gone back on me. You said you would like to come out of course I would like to have you but I would rather you would wait until I go home & visit out there as I would like to have you see what my home is like I think I shall go home before very much longer. Well Good bye for this time and write soon
from your friend
Stella

The Chautauqua Lake hotels are serviced by both railroad and steamboat. Norman's letters from Maple Springs will illustrate hotel experience on the lake late in the century. The Maple Springs Hotel was small compared to the several major resorts then operating. "Aunt" Addie Cobb is Edith's mother and a sort of surrogate aunt to Martie and Mattie's friends.

Maple Springs, Chaut. Co, N.Y.,
June 6 1893
Dear freind Stella,
I will now try and answer your kind and welcome letter which I received nearly one week ago. I was very glad to hear you are well and hope you may continue so. Well I have hired out for the summer at my Aunts here at Maple Springs as I presume you have guessed before this from the heading of this letter. It is not just the kind of work I would like best, but I thought I would like it better than farming. I get $22 per month. My Uncle, Mr. Francis is a very nice man to work for I think. He keeps 35 or 40 boarders during the summer but has only 3 now excepting when fishermen come and stay a day or two. I came here 2 weeks ago next Thursday, Was home Sunday, went down on a Steamboat and returned Monday morning on the train. I think this a very pleasant place. it is situated about three miles from Chautauqua on the opposite side of the lake. Aunt Addie is working at George's this summer. Mrs. Gertie Goldstien is here at work also Laura Hayes (whom you have heard the Dorne girls speak of I presume.) and Rosetta Lewis is coming here the first of July. That makes me think she mailed a letter here yesterday directed to you which you will probably recieve the same time as this. Have you heard from home lately? and when do you think you will go home? I would like very much to visit you there but am afraid it will be impossible as I shall have to stay here untill September Well it is getting very late so I will close for this time
write very soon
Your loving freind
Norman

Sparta
June 15th 1893
Dear Stella
Your kind letter was received tuesday evening I was a good deal
disapointed in not getting a letter from you last saturday so I
went down tuesday I was verry glad to hear that you and Irva
was coming home you tel Irva to pay your fair and I will pay
him tel him to come perpard to stay a weak and you must stay til
the first of September Dot and I ar going this after noon to the
Baker grave to picnic now dont fail to answer this and come no I
guess you better rite and let me know when to meat you at the
train
your Father
F.W. Murdock
the widow miller was thrown from her buggy last Sunday
evening near Alonzo Murdock's and badly hirt she is at Alonzo's
yet cant move herself in bed dont fail to come and stay

Du Bois, Pa.,
June 20th, 1893
Tuesday Morning
Dear friend Norman
I will now try and answer your letter which I read some time ago
and will make no excuses for not writing sooner only that I have
been quite busy. Well I hope you are enjoying yourself at your
new place of work. I think it must be somewhat cooler there than
it is here I would not care if I were near a lake these warm days.
How is Rosseta getting along I rec'd her letter same time I did
yours & she said she had not been very well, tell her I mean to
answer it before long. Last night was Firemans parade it being
the fifth Anniversary of the great fire in DuBois, it was quite
good I thought. Arrangements are being made for a grand celebration here the 4th. I am going home I guess about the middle
or last of next month I rec'd a letter from home to come now and
stay until 1st of Sept. but guess I will wait a few more weeks so
that I will be at home when Mr. Griesemer is at the worlds fair he
will go in Sept I guess. Lulu is taking music lessons seems to be

learning quite fast I guess. Well as there is nothing much to write-
I will close for this time hoping to hear from you soon.
I am your sincere friend
Stella

*Chicago's Columbia Exposition, the four hundredth anniversary of Columbus'
voyage to America, adversely affected the 1893 season at Chautauqua Lake.*

Maple Springs, Chaut. Co, N.Y.
June 25 1893
Sunday Afternoon
Dear friend Stella,
I received your "as ever" welcome letter last Wednesday, and will
now try and steal a few minutes in which to answer it. This has
been a rainy day thus far but we have been having some very fine
weather of late I think it must be very warm in DuBois, is it not?
We are very busy here at present getting ready for the summer season although uncle Smith anticipates a dull season on account of
the Columbian Exposition. Rosetta Lewis came here to work last
Sunday but was obliged to go home Wednesday morn on account
of a lame arm. Rheumatism she thought it was. The Royal Templars
hold their annual Picnic at this place next Tuesday and we expect a
very busy day if it is pleasant Friday night there was a man here
wishing to go to Chaut. and he missed the boat so I rowed him
over. started about 20 minutes of 9 and got back at 10 p.m. 4 miles
from here to Chaut. I hope you can attend church more regularly
than I do for it is impossible here to go to church, Sunday being the
busiest day in the week Which of the churches do you attend mostly? I think if you keep putting off going home you will soon make
the time Xmas but if you are home in Sept and nothing unusual
happens I think I shall come and see you then. What do you expect
to do the 4th of July? I think I shall be found at Maple Springs
working no doubt. Well I have spoiled all the news I can think of so
I will close for this time hoping this will find you well and happy
I remain
Your Sincere Friend
Norman
P.S. Write sooner than before
N.W.I.

P.E. (Phil) Griesemer is John's brother. He begins work at the studio as an artist but will eventually take John's place as manager. Fourth of July events are briefly described in the two following letters.

Du Bois, Pa.
July 6th '93.
Dear Friend Norman: –
How do you do this evening and what for a time did you have the 4th. I had a midling good time. the parades were very good I thought and the town was decorated very nice. It is raining here to-night, yesterday we had a terrible wind storm together with thunder and lightning several buildings showed the effects a few were blown over and some struck by lightning. Irva & Eliza went to Bradford Sat. morning and did not return until Tues. eve. they took Lulu with them and left the two youngest with me I had a good time all to myself keeping house Was sorry Rosetta had to leave her place Do you see Martie & Mat. very often. I have got my mind made up now to go home a week from Sat. and unless I do as you say "put it off until Xmas" think I will go then or soon after. What kind of work do you have to do? I suppose you have a good many boat rides Mr. Griesemers brother is here now working for him. He is a good artist, has been married but a short time. I suppose you have lots of fun where you are work-ing, do you have as much as we did picking grapes, I hope so at least. I often think of the many queer things that happened dur-ing those few week's for instance the evening we all spent at Mr. Pecks. Well it is late so I will close for this time, don't for pity sake let any one read this I don't know when I ever made so many mistakes writing
Good night
Stella
(Write soon)

Charlie Parker works on Pa's farm in Sparta. He is the brother of Edna Parker Frost, who will be mentioned in future letters. Charlie worked the grape fields with Norman and Stella in 1892.

Maple Springs
July 14
Friday Eve.
Dear friend Stella,
How do you do this evening. you are expected to go home to-morrow I suppose well I wish you a safe Journey and a pleasant visit. This is a very pleasant eve at Maple Springs I think it is very warm in Du Bois now is it not. Rosetta is here at work again and she and another young lady Miss Owen That works here and I have just been out rowing. Yes? I do have a good many boat rides and quite a good time but not as good as we had at Portland though. You asked what for a time I had the 4th Well I had a Picnic in every sense of the word, That is there was a picnic came here from Jamestown and we were very busy all day waiting on them. They had a dance of course and stayed till Midnight and I did not get to bed until 1 o'clock in the morning Martie and Rosetta came here together and took dinner and then they went on the Steamer to Long Point which is about 1 mile south of here, where there was a big celebration they came back here about 11 o'clock and Mart stayed with me until morning He is not very well this summer not been able to do any hard work at all. I was up to Mr. Watermans one week ago last Sunday and that was the first time I had seen Mattie for 4 or 5 months at least she was wondering why she did not get a letter from you The work I have to do here is not very easy I have to do every thing from handling baggage and renting row boats to dressing fish & chicken As it is getting late I will close for this time. Give my regards to your father & the Dorne girls if you see them and tell Charlie Parker Hello!
Good Night
Your sincere friend
 Norman
write soon and all the news from Sparta
"N.W.I."

Stella returns to Sparta. Her older brother Will lives with his wife, Rose Weaver Murdock, in the village close to the train station. Pa's farm is about three miles away. Rosetta Lewis is Martie Waterman's sometimes sweetheart.

Spartansburg, Pa.
7 28 '93
Friend Norman.
Your letter received contents noted I came home last Tuesday evening Irva came home with me. We started Monday noon got about 4 miles this side of Kane where we came to a freight train wreck and had to wait at Kane from four until eleven got to Sparta at about two and stayed at my brothers there until Tuesday evening One man had his leg broken in the wreck. It seems good to get home again after being away so long Pa has not got through haying yet We have two hired men now and expect another next week I have not seen Charlie yet. Ida Harrington the girl that is working for us Says "Give his love to me" She ment give him my love. Tell Rosetta that I am going to write to her before long I am glad she is better How is your brother and sisters folks getting along I would like to see those little girls. It is quite cold here to day for July. There is being a new M.E. Church built about a mile from us. Well news are scarce with me as usual so I will close hoping to hear from you soon.
From your friend Stella Murdock
Spartansburg Pa.

Panama Rocks is a dramatic geological formation made from ocean quartz and suitable for climbing and exploration. The "Rocks" are a popular Chautauqua County attraction.

Maple Springs
Aug 6 – 1893
Dear friend, –
I received your kind and welcome letter last Monday. Was glad to hear you was at home and that Irva came with you for I know it is anything but pleasant to travel alone. Everything is very quiet here. I think this is the dullest season I ever knew on Chaut. Lake. We only

have about 10 Boarders and expect 2 of them will soon leave. Martie & Rosetta & Mattie and a fellow by the name of Fred Smith went for a drive to Panama-Rocks yesterday. I never was there but it is on the other side of the lake about 10 miles from here I think. Rosetta is not coming back to work any more as Aunt Minnie thinks it is too hard for her. How long do you intend to stay at Sparta? I do not intend to work here after the first of Sept. and if nothing happens shall be down soon after providing you are at home How is your fathers health this summer? I hope better than when at Du Bois last winter. I dont have a chance to go home or any where very much while here as Sunday is nearly the busiest day of the week and I havent been in a church in nearly 3 months. I think when I am through here I'll not hire out where it is necessary to work Sundays again. It seems as though news never was as scarce as this Afternoon so I will close this hoping you will excuse my penmanship and write very soon.
I remain as ever your
Sincere friend
Norman

Stella's mother, Mary Ann (Mate) Murdock, died suddenly November 11, 1883 (letter, Nov. 11, 1893). Stella's stepmother Dorothy (Dot) will be mentioned frequently in letters to come. Pa is a member of the Odd Fellows.

Spartansburg, Pa.
Aug. 22 1893.
Dear friend Norman
Your Epistle of Aug 6th came to hand in due season and its contents read with pleasure the only fault I had to find with it was-it was like the most of mine are apt to be a little too short. I have been having a very enjoyable time since I came home going to picnics meeting some of my old friends, etc. I say going to picnics I haven't been to but one although I think that was attended by as many people as some three or four are sometimes. It was at a place called Willis Grove, about fourteen miles from here last Sat. A lady friend of mine and my-self went together and from there we went to Cambridge a nice little town having several mineral springs about 19 miles from here, stayed there over Sunday with my step mothers brother's

people and came home last evening. I attended church both morning and evening. Well I suppose you will soon have a vacation from work, I suppose you have no other place in view as yet I hope you may have the luck to find a position that suits you better than the one you have now seems to. When do you think you can come out? I think I will be at home until about the 1st of Oct. There is going to be an Odd Fellows Picnic at Lake Canadohta, which is about six miles from us the 31st of this month wish you could be here to go but suppose that would be rather impossible would it not? Do you know whether Rosetta rec'd my letter or not? I addressed it to Maple Springs, thinking she was there yet. Are Rosetta & Martie going together again? I saw Ethie and Nora the other day they think they will go to pick grapes about the first of Sept.
Well I will close for this time.
Good by.
Stella.

Norman's first visit to Sparta. Since he is working on George's farm, he is free to travel. He will take the Western New York and Pennsylvania Railroad which has a depot in Spartansburg. His visit lasted from September 2 to September 8.

Fluvanna, N.Y.
Aug 30 – 1893
Dear freind Stella
I received your kind letter last Monday morn and was glad to hear you are having such a good time. I wish it might have been possible for me to have been with you at the picnic tommorow but am glad to say that if nothing happens I will be at Sparta Sat. next September second I have not been at Maple Springs since two weeks ago last Mon. and am now working for George. George and Kate are away visiting friends near Brocton went away yesterday and will not be back untill tomorrow sometime. "Aunt Ada" Cobb is here staying so we are running the ranch alone you see It is getting late bedtime and I will close this saving all other news untill I see you I think I shall come on the train starting from Mayville about 11 a.m. Sept 2.
Please! dont censure me too hardly for this short letter
good Night
Norman

*Norman has spent the last week with Stella. Intimations in his letters of
November 5 and November 20 suggest that the visit didn't pass well. Stella
will take the Western New York and Pennsylvania Railroad to Corry, then
transfer to the Erie to arrive in Jamestown on October 17. She stays long
enough to visit with Norman, several of his relatives, and their mutual friends.
Norman is uncharacteristically late and rather impersonal in his short letter to
her following her return to Dubois.*

Fluvanna N.Y.
Sept. 10-1893.
Sunday
Dear freind Stella.
I now take pen in hand to let you know that I am still among the
living. I arrived home safely Friday night about six and improved
the time yesterday digging potatoes Aunt Addie and I are here
alone today George and Kate having gone up the lake driving. It
seems more like August than Sept. today it is so warm and still
just right for a ride on the lake. I have not heard from Martie
since before I came to Penna. I expected to get a letter from him
before this but I guess he has forgotten his old chum. Well what
did your people say about my forgetting my satchel? George says
I left it to make an excuse to come again but I think our freindship is a sufficient excuse when I see fit to come, don't you? I
hope you will hurry and get your sewing done so as to have time
to come this way when you go to DuBois. I think if you come by
the way of Jamestown it will cost less than it will to come
through Mayville and if you will write in time I will be glad to
meet you at Jamestown.
Sunday Evening
I will now try and finish this letter which I began this morning
Aunt Addie and I have just been up to my sisters this evening
they are going to have a nice house when it is finished We drove
our 3 year old colt and a new buggy George bought yesterday
quite a good looking rig "you bet." Well news are scarce and
besides it is nearly half past nine and although you are not here
to send me to bed I will say good night & write soon
Your sincere freind
Norman

Uncle Lon (Alonzo Murdock) is Pa's brother. He and his wife, Jennie, live on the Murdock family farm about a mile from Pa's farm.

Spartansburg, Pa.
Sep 23 1893.
Dear Friend Norman

I have made up my mind that it is about time I should answer that letter of about two weeks ago. Was glad to hear you reached home all safely and hope you are better of your cold by this time. Do you realize much benefit from your medicine that is here? I have about made up my mind to go that way back and so thought if you are in no hurry for your satchel it would be better to wait and bring it instead of sending it. I can't tell now how soon I will go but within two or three weeks I think. Eliza and the children are here now. we went over to my Uncle Lon's yesterday and from there to my cousin Weldon Davis's and stayed over night. After you went that day I stayed to Edna's for supper and then took Ida Frost over home and did not get back until after dark. Ida Harrington has gone to her school I think your brother is quite mistaken about your leaving your satchel for an excuse to come back instead I have got it for an excuse to go there that is if I don't care what I say. One of my old school mates who has been married only about two years and lived in Oil City died a short time ago of typhoid fever and was brought here for burial I attended her funeral and it was very sad she was so young and the only girl her parents had she had three brothers here and one in the west. they took it real hard. I hear that Willie Botts & his sister have gone to pick grapes how I wish I had went. Ida Frost has also gone. Pa is not as lame now as while you were here but is not entirely over it yet he is not a bit well Riley Parker (Charlie's brother) and wife have been out visiting. Well I did not go to the Corry fair as I intended My folks did not go and so I thought I wouldn't Pa is getting ready to go to town so I will bring my letter to a close for this time hoping to hear from you soon I am your sincere friend.
S.M.M.
P.S. I hope you will excuse the many mistakes in this letter

Fluvanna, N.Y.
Oct. 3, 1893.
Tuesday eve.
Dear freind Stella. –
I received your letter last Wednesday and was glad to hear you
are coming. I have been working quite steadily since I came
home haven't missed but one day, and then I was obliged to go
to Jamestown Havent seen Martie since I came home but received
a letter from him. He is in school at Sinclairsville a small town
about like Sparta. I suppose you know that Mattie is picking
grapes I'll "bet" she is having a good time dont you? but then did
you ever see her when she wasnt having a good time? I cant help
but think how different things are to night than they were a year
ago but then "such is life." We have just finished digging potatoes and began husking corn to day. Will have about 800 or 900
bushels at least. Well? I can't think of much to write so I will
close hoping to hear from you soon and see you sooner.
I remain as ever
Your freind Norman.

Stella's Uncle Siles is a maternal relation.

Jamestown N.Y.
Tuesday 17th
Dear Friend Norman
I came here to my Uncle Sile's this morning. You may come after
me about Thursday I guess if you can as well as not - hoping to
see you soon will say good by for this time,
Stella
They live at 208 East-2d St go up two flights of stairs.
(If you haven't the time to spare and think you can't find me I
can come on the cars.)

From Rosetta Lewis.

Dewittville
Oct. 23 1893
My Dear Friend
I will now try and ans. your ever welcome letter which I received
while at Brocton. I just returned yesterday I did not see the Dorn girls
once I was not down to Brocton only once while I was there I wanted
to get over and see them and Mr. and Mrs. Martin but my intension
did not last me. I had lots of fun this Fall. there was too girls besides
me and the lady of the house. the girls names were Ettie Brown and
Maggie Harden. Ettie was from Greenvill Penn. and the other from
Cleveland O. they were both very nice. I began school this morning
we have a gentleman teacher we like him very much what are you
doing now days to pass the time away. I have not seen or heard anything of Norman in a long time, only once since I got through work
at the Springs. Mattie is to Portland yet. I have not seen her in a dogs
age. I will forget how she looks. If I did not have her pictures to lok at
once in a while Martin is going to Sinclearvill to school now I have
not seen him to speak to him since I got back from the convention. he
and I have dissolved partnership again and for good this time but
dont mention it to anyone for my sake. well I am rather tired and
guess I will close hoping to hear from you soon
I remain as ever your true friend
Rosetta Lewis

Dewittville, N.Y.
Nov 5 – 93
Sunday Eve
Dear freind Stella, –
I will now write you a few lines. I am now staying here at Mr.
Brown's near father's helping him cut wood. I meant to write sooner
but kept neglecting it. I suppose you are at Du Bois again by this
time. how do you like the new store? It is much better than the old
one I suppose Pa was at the World's Fair just one week from the day
you left Jamestown He told about going up in the Masonic Temple
which is about 300 feet high and contains 21 stories quite a high
building isnt' it. Mattie has returned from the grape country so I hear

and Rosetta Lewis is at her home in Dewittville at least I saw her there the other day as I drove past Well as it is bedtime and news is very scarce I will close hoping to hear from you soon.
Your freind
Norman Ingerson

Jamestown's Boat Landing, 1890s.
Track crossing Chadaskoin River leads to Celeron.
Track in foreground leads to Lakewood.
Johnson's Ice Co. (three barns) in background.

III

Well! I have hired out for the season to Johnson's Ice Co. delivering ice

Any disappointment Norman may have felt during Stella's visit must have been minor. Stella all but ignores the curt tone of Norman's letter following the visit. Her personable, chatty response (Nov. 11, 1893) assures Norman that all is well. Even so, the matter seems serious enough to Norman to warrant an apology.

The two will not see each other again for fourteen months. During that time Stella is often, and Norman occasionally, negligent in answering letters. Their correspondence is nothing less than a courtship, but the courtship in 1894 continues secondary to the routine of their daily lives. Norman accepts employment with the Johnson Ice Co., a position he seems to feel appropriate to the pursuit of middle class success. His callow, self-confidence is rather endearing, and the energy of his pursuit never falters. Stella, now integral to life in the Murdock household in Dubois, feels no more independent than she did a year previously. She approaches life cautiously. Her experimentation with a bicycle ends abruptly after a fall. She manages to purchase an air brush but never learns how to use it. Often, she is homesick for Sparta. Norman and Stella's lives begin to mirror the inexorable routine of the days they are chronicling. Their meeting at the opening of 1895 is sealed auspiciously with a kiss.

Mt. Jewett, McKean County, lies about twenty miles south of Bradford and is a major railroad junction. Stella transferred from the Erie to the Buffalo, Rochester, and Pittsburg line at Bradford. Dubois is forty miles south of Mt. Jewett. The new studio is at the heart of the business district. Phil Griesemer is now the manager.

DuBois, Pa.

Nov 11th 1893

Dear friend Norman:

Received your welcome, but very short letter the other day. I had almost come to the conclusion that you were not going to write at all. I stayed at my Uncles in Mt Jewett a little over a week. I had a lovely visit there and in fact at all of the places which I went. It has been nearly four weeks since I came from home and havent heard a word from there since. Don't you think they are good ones? How does it happen you are not at your brothers: I suppose you enjoyed the week at your Aunts as well as expected. How is your cousin that was sick while I was there did he get well? Questions till you cant rest. Irva is at Warren canvassing this week, I think he will go out home to stay over Sunday. He has been to the Worlds Fair. I like our new store much better than where we was. I have been making draperies and keeping books since I came back, draperies for sale pictures this time. Well I haven't been to any dances yet and don't intend to go to any very soon. What's the use of belonging to a church if you cant live up to the rules of it. By the way have you been to church since we went that Sunday? I went twice while in Mt. Jewett but not at all since I came back. Suppose you can see Mattie and Martie quite often now can you not. I think Mattie might write to me. I am writing at the store and am all alone it being quitting time for Saturday night. I did not tell you Irva's folks have moved. When I came I was somewhat surprised to find the house all empty and so came up to the store and they had gone to supper and then I began to inquire where they lived and found that they had moved on that same horrid old street just the other side of Mr. Berringer there is a house just a few steps from us on both sides and it makes the rooms so very dark. Did you ever see finer weather this time a year than we are having now, how I did want

to be out to day, it makes me think of the days I drove so much while at home. I was almost home sick Sunday but will not have much time for that only Sundays. Did your brother think you had gone on to Bradford that day? When I got to Bradford my train was waiting and I did not have time to even get a ticket. I think it seems too bad for you to go to cutting wood after fitting your-self for something better. but perhaps you will be able to get a position after while. I hope so at least. Most any kind of work is better than nothing I think. It is just 10 years ago to-day since Ma died and a good deal such a day if I remember rightly. Well I am beginning to feel as though it was supper time. I guess you will think it is better to write a short letter than one full of trifles and nonsense like this. Good night for this time Write soon and a good long letter
Stella.
I don't know where to address this but I suppose to DeWittville. So here goes.

From Mattie Waterman.

DeWittville N.Y.
Nov. 19. 1893
Dear Stella
I guess you will think I have entirely forgotten you but I have not I think of you often and wish I could see you and I was so sorry I was not at home when you and Norman were there I nearly cried but I thought perhaps that would not do any good but I want to see you so bad wish you could come out again wish I could come out there but dont suppose I can. And but I wish you would have your picture taken and send to me. We are having lovely weather here or have been It isnt so good this afternoon it is snowing dreadfully and blowing a perfect gale so awfully cold. winter I guess pretty soon. Mart is going to school at Sinclairsville has been driving from home quite a while but guess he will have to board away now. I had a lovely time at Portland this fall wish you had been there I saw Nora and Ethie while there they seemed just as they used to I guess there was a larger crowd at

Mr. Martin's this fall than last fall. Mr. Martin doesnt drink anymore I am glad of that. Well I guess I cant think of anything
worth writing so had better stop hoping to hear from you soon I
remain your sincere Friend
Mattie
P.S. Wish we were at Portland just a little while all together again
I have been to church at Dentons wish you had been there ans.
soon
M.W.

Dewittville
Nov 20 93
Dear friend Stella –
I received your welcome letter last Tuesday and was glad to
know you arrived home safely. I don't wonder you thought it
strange I would write such a short letter as my last was but to tell
the truth I was afraid that the shorter it was the better it would
please you. but now I hope and believe that is not true At least!
forgive me for that and I will do better hereafter. Well I am still
cutting wood but dont you think it is because I like the business
for it is not. yet to say the least it is honorable and I can make
from 4 to 5 dollars per week which I think is better than nothing
and I still hope I shall find something better soon. I was down
home Saturday and stayed till last night. My cousin that was sick
is much better and they think he will be well. I went to
Jamestown Saturday the first time since the day you went away.
It was not much such a day as that was though for the roads are
muddy now and it was much colder. We had a severe snowstorm
last week. enough snow fell so that people went with sleighs one
day, but it is nearly all gone now. Georges folks are going to
move in the Spring they don't know where yet, but think some of
moving on to a farm 2 or 3 miles from Bemus Point back away
from the lake. He and I are talking some (providing I find no
suitable position before Spring) of going into partnership and
then I would have a home for 1 year at least. That morning after I
left you at the train I came back through the depot and George

was just driving down there looking for me and he was already
to go. We got home just in time for dinner then I took the
Afternoon train to Dewittville. I was at my Aunts just a week Pa
returned from Chicago the next Monday after you left I got
through the week there better than I expected but I was so busy I
did not have time to get lonesome. I haven't been to church but
once since you were here nor been up to Mr. Waterman's since
we were there Think I shall go up there next Sunday and go to
church too I presume Wish you could be there too I don't think I
would have much time to get homesick do you? I have quite a
good place to board "Brown" is the peoples name. they are quite
plain but very jolly and they have no children some different
than the place I boarded at last winter I stopped at my sisters last
night on my way home they are not entirely settled yet but more
so than that night we stopped there. How are your folks at home
getting along? I suppose you have heard from them before this?
Well it is nearly 10 P.M. and I am "just a little" sleepy so I will
close for this time.
Write very soon
"Good night"
Norman

*The 1893 depression was largely a result of political wrangling over monetary
policy. "Wheel" is the popular period term for a bicycle. Riding became a
national obsession toward the end of the nineteenth century. Mark and Frances
Cheney are settling in to their new home. Stella's twenty-first birthday,
November 29, 1893, passes nearly unremarked.*

DuBois, Pa.
Dec 4th 93
Dear Friend Norman
Yours of the 20th at hand and contents noted, will try and scrib-
ble you a few lines this evening, but the children are so noisy
don't know as I can think of much to write. Will you except a let-
ter written with a lead pencil I am writing at the house and the
ink is all up to the studio and thought I must write to-night.
Where did you spend Thanksgiving at Mr. Browns I suppose.
Irva is at home now has just been reading a piece about the many

people that are out of work and are in want. I should think the Democrats would be satisfied this time. Well if I am not careful I may find my-self talking polotics. I received a letter from Pa the other day. I wrote to him while in Mt. Jewett and he thought I would write again when I got to DuBois said he worried about me until Irva came home, did I tell you in my last letter he had been home? He said he dreamed he had to shoot me for something. Only three weeks from to day until Christmas, how time flies and not so very fast either when I think of how long it will probably be until I go home J.M. Griesmeyer the single one has gone to Chicago to see his sister who is very sick My Aunt in Mt Jewett sent me a very pretty photograph case for a birthday present I suppose you think you will soon be your own boss I dont know that I feel any more independent than I did a year ago. I got a letter from Mattie at last. Did you go up there the day you spoke of going, is her cousin there yet Have you sleighing now there is a little here to day but I guess that wheels go the best Derwood and Mate have gone to bed and it is about 10 o'clock, Lulu dressed up in Derwood's clothes and went over to Mr Berringers I did not tell you I was getting the large sum of $2 a week that does not seem like very much after spending so much? I think it is all I earn now and am in hopes of being able to earn more after while
Give my best regards to Georges folks and write soon
Good night
Stella

The eve of Norman's twenty-first birthday. Plans for Christmas are under way. A.L. Waterman is Martie and Mattie's father. Denton's is a crossroads, the site of a schoolhouse and church, a few miles east of Dewittville.

A Merry Christmas
Fluvanna, N.Y.
Dec., 18 – 93
Dear Freind –
I received your letter nearly two weeks ago, but have been very neglectful in regard to answering it. I thought perhaps I had better write to night as this would be the last chance before attaining

my majority although I dont anticipate any particular difference in feeling (as you said) after I am 21. I thought of you on your birthday and would have been glad to have sent you something more substantial than mere thoughts as a reminder but that was hardly possible. I have been at home nearly a month now. did not spend Thanksgiving at Mr Brown's but at Mr. A. L. Waterman's had a very good time was there the Sunday after and stayed and carried Martie to School Monday - then came home next day and have been here mostly ever since. "Aunt" Addie and Eddith Cobb came when I did and are here now Edith sends you her best wishes for a merry Xmas. Mattie is staying at home now she goes to School at Dentons. there is to be a Christmas-Tree there next Sat. Eve. I think I shall be there, as I intend to spend Christmas with Martie. Edith will go home then (to her uncle Asa's) or at least she intends to now. Georges people are going up to Kate's Mother's Xmas so you see this will be a rather deserted place then. we are going to move the first of Mar. to the place I spoke of in my last letter, George and I are cutting wood (some of the time) near my Sisters so we carry our dinner and eat there. I am talking of trying the Teacher's Examination next Spring. We have had some good sleighing but there is none now it is snowing to day though, hope there will be enough for Sleighing Christmas. You will be at Irva's then I suppose, hope you may have a good time and lots of presents. Dont wait as long as I did before answering this letter. I will close and write to Martin

"Good night,"

Norman.

Ida Harrington is Stella's friend from Sparta. Ida sometimes hires out to work for Pa during harvests.

Du Bois
Dec. 29 – 93.
Dear Friend Norman: –
Thought I would write you a few lines this morning in answer to your letter of about one week ago. I suppose you had a merry Christmas at Mr. Wattermans. I hope so We were invited out to dinner but Eliza and Lulu were both sick and so we couldn't go. I went to an entertainment at the church in the evening, haven't been working at the studio since a week ago to day but think Eliza will be well enough so I can by Monday. There is a great deal of sickness here now. So many are having the grip or pneumonia and several have died with it. What did you get Christmas? I got a manicure set, a pair of velvet house slippers, a box of oil paints & brushes and a breast pin. I will send you a tie for New Years intended it for Xmas but didn't get it done in time. I made one for Irva too. I suppose Ida Harrington was married the 27th to Frank Firth of Philadelphia I would liked very much to have attended her wedding but couldn't very well. We are having very muddy rainy weather here at present Have you been out skating any this winter? I am thinking of learning if the ice ever freezes up again. I sent you one of my photos some time ago but suppose you did not get it as I addressed it to DeWittville. I can think of nothing more to write and so will close and write home. Write soon and all the news
from your friend Stella.
(Good by)

Norman's letter dated January 7, 1894, is missing. Stella's answer is nearly a month in coming. Nora Dorne from Sparta is married and will henceforth be separated from her sister Ethie. Franklin Murdock, Will and Rose's third child, is born. Pa's grim humor regarding his namesake will prove prophetic.

DuBois, Pa.
Feb 2 1894
Dear friend Norman:
Will scribble you a few lines this evening in answer to yours of the 7th ult. How are you and all your people by this time? Eliza & Mate went to Spartansburg Tuesday to attend her cousins Mrs James Haydon's funeral and I am house keeper. The two children and I stayed alone one night but Irva is at home now so we are not so lonesome. We are having sleighing here now about the first real good sleighing we have had this winter but I don't enjoy it much my-self. I hear Nora is married. Suppose she will not go to the grape country anymore. We had quite a fire here about the 13th I think it was. We were staying with Mrs. Hollister and had not retired yet when the alarm was given at about 12 o'clock. It broke out in Grier Brothers hardware store and had gotten under quite a headway in the hotel across from the new bank building they were putting up while you were here, before it was put out. No I have not been ice skating yet it is getting so late now don't know as it will pay me to get any for all I would skate. I may though if it keeps cold long one of our neighbor girls and I have been talking of learning. I got Mattie's picture all right but haven't sent her mine yet guess she will begin to think my word is not very good but I had given them away but one and keep neglecting having any more made. My brother Wills folks have another boy Pa wrote that he thought it would die sometime as they were going to call it Frank after him. Well! news are scarce so good night for this time
your sincere friend
S.M.M.
(Write soon. Do not wait as long as I did)

Johnson's Ice Co. was one of several firms on Chautauqua Lake that harvested ice for sale during the warm months. Its barn stood just up from the boat landing and the Chautauqua Lake Railway depot toward Fluvanna. According to the 1893 Jamestown City Directory, Herman Johnson lived at 500 West Seventh Street. He probably owned a second property at 504 where Norman boarded. The houses are two blocks from the boat landing, within walking distance to the barn. Frances Cheney's second child, Ralph, is born. Her husband Mark has a daughter, Alice, by a previous marriage.

Jamestown N.Y.
Feb 25 – 94
Dear freind Stella,
I will now answer yours of about two weeks ago. Should have written before but have been very busy. Well! I have hired out for the season to Johnson Ice Co delivering ice. began about two weeks ago of course we dont deliver much ice now but are harvesting the crop for next summer I did not choose this work because it was just what I wanted but because it pays quite a fair salary. I am to receive $20 per month & board till the 1st of May and $25 for the next 6 months. There are 3 others working for the Company now one of them boards here with me at Mr. Johnson's "one of the firm."
Havent been home for two weeks. George's people were all well then. Howard (the baby) was just commencing to walk but he doesn't talk any yet. I think Mildred can talk enough for both though. My sister has got a new boy about 4 weeks old. I havent heard from Mr. Waterman's since I was there Christmas suppose Martin is attending school the same as ever though. Yes! I have heard that Martie's cousin Edith Cobb was going to teach school near there next summer. I was at the Methodist church this afternoon and heard a very good sermon I am thinking some of joining the Y.M.C.A. before long but havent fully decided yet. We have been having some intensely cold weather of late last night the mercury fell to 10 below zero and friday night it was four below we also are having good sleighing but like yourself I dont enjoy it much I suppose before I go home again George's folks will have moved; as they are going March 1st. Well! I will close for this time and please dont wait as long as I before answering.
Your sincere freind
Norman Ingerson
504 West Seventh St.

Another month between letters. Norman, perhaps, is wondering. The studio's success enables Irva to purchase a home. The Pennsylvania Grit is nearby Williamsport's newspaper.

April 3d 1894.
Dear friend Norman: –
I have been intending to answer your welcome letter for a long time but keep neglecting it and so thought I must write to night. Edith Zeigler, a neighbor girl of ours and I have been up to Mr. Griesemers spending the evening and as it is now after 10 o'clock I will not promise you a very long letter. Well! how are you and all your folks and how do you like your new work by this time? I suppose you do not deliver any ice yet. Irva is away from home as usual don't expect him back until the last of the month he has sold his place in Spartansburg to Pa and bought a house and lot here. It is on top of the hill nearly 1/2 mile I guess from the studio. I am afraid I will not like it very well it will be so far to walk would not mind it so much if there was not such a hill to climb but will be glad to get away from this place anway. We expect to move as soon as Irva comes home. There was a man murdered here on main street a week or so ago, perhaps you have read about it. There was an account of it in the Grit. The last I heard from home Pa and Dot were both about sick. Marva Murdock is working for him he is a distant cousin of mine. You spoke of joining the Y.M.C.A. I think it a good idea hope you will. There is going to be a fair here for the benefit of the fire company evenings of next week Wish you were here and could go. I think it will be good. Did you notice the Northern Lights last Friday eve It looked lovely from here. Some thought it was not the Northern Lights but a warning of something. Well! Norman I cant think of much to write, think if I could see you could talk enough though. I must close for this time answer as soon as you get this and I think I will surely answer sooner next time.
Good night,
Stella

George and Kate have moved to their new farm outside Bemus Point. The "Point" is ten short stops from Jamestown on the Chautauqua Lake Railway. The "small steamers" Norman mentions are the "Celeron" and "Greenhurst," named for lakeside communities on opposites sides of the lower lake. They were purchased at the Columbia Exposition by Jamestown's most prominent nineteenth century entrepreneurs, the Broadhead family. The Broadheads were in the process of constructing Celeron Park, soon to be mentioned in the letters.

Jamestown, N.Y.
Apr 8 –94
Sunday
Dear freind Stella, –
Your Welcome letter received last Thursday found me well as usual and I hope this may find you the same. Mr. Johnson and wife have gone out to visit a neighbor leaving myself and the other fellow (Mr Hotchkiss who also works here) alone. So I think I will take this period of quiet to write to you Well I like my work even better than on the start. They (the J.I. Co.) are nice pleasant people and I think if I do my duty we shall get along very nicely. No! I havent delivered any ice yet but expect to begin some time this month. They have just begun building a barn so you may imagine we all have enough to keep us out of mischief. I was at my brothers the third week in march taking a vacation. they were all as well as usual and like their new home first rate I think. In some respects it is better than where they lived before and in some not so good. He has one of the best barns in the township but the house is not as good in proportion although it is better than the other. Of course I went up to Martin's and made a visit. He is still going to school but talks of teaching next fall. Shouldn't think he could keep sober long enough to make a good schoolteacher would you? Mattie is staying at home now and her cousin Miss Cobb is teaching school near my aunts where we called that day. Pa is not going to stay there this summer but says he is going to Iowa very soon he was at George's when I was there I wish he could stay there but I suppose he knows better what he wants than I do. Haven't we had queer weather this Spring though. I hope it will come warm again soon anyhow. There have been two small steamers running on the lake since two weeks ago rather cool for a trip on the lake dont you

think so? I wish we might attend church together this evening if nothing happens I think I shall go just the same. Well! Stella I've scribbled away here for over half an hour and haven't said much of interest either but if I could be with you I believe I would enjoy talking much better than writing; but that is not possible as I dont expect a single holiday this summer. I am very thankful though because I shall not have to work Sundays I hope you will like your new home and hope climbing the hill will not be to hard for you also that you may attend the fair of which you spoke and have a good time.

good bye for this time

Norman

write sooner

Stella appears never to have mastered portraiture. She left a single landscape in oil now in the possession of Jenn Elvgren. Norman met Stella's aunt, wife of Uncle Siles, when Stella visited Jamestown the previous fall.

Du Bois, Pa.

April 29th 94.

Dear Friend: –

Your welcome letter of the 8th at hand. How are you spending this pleasant Sunday? I went to church this forenoon and was intending to go to the woods this afternoon but the girl I was going with did not come and so I thought I would write to you. Irva & Eliza went up to Mr. Griesemers and I have been alone most all the afternoon. We have not moved yet but expect to next week I am glad you like your work I get rather sick of mine sometimes & wish I was back home. I intend getting me an air brush as soon as possible and then when I learn to use it I can make more money. Jack is going to leave us. He and another man are going into business in Scranton this state. It is a place ten times as large as this he is going Tuesday It will seem rather odd at the studio without him. I suppose they will get another artist after while. Times are so hard now that we do not have as much work as we did. Do you ever see my Aunt in Jamestown? I suppose you would not know her if you did, having met her only the once. I have not written to her since I came back guess she will think I am a good rude but I am not a very good correspon- der as you know. I wish you could come out this Summer but suppose you can't take the time. The fair here was very good I went three nights. The last evening I was there they had a min- strel play and the opera house was crowded. I was afraid it might go down. The paper stated that there was the most in it that there ever was before even the stage was crooked. I sat in the galery and was not very sorry when I got down. Well! I have written a long letter of nothing as usual. Will close for this time hoping to hear from you soon

from your sincere friend

Stella.

I don't know as you can read this horrid writing my pen is so poor.

Good Bye

Write Soon

S.M.M.

Jamestown N.Y.

May 6 1894

3 p.m.

Dear freind,

How do you do? All of the household having departed for the time being; I am pleased to take this hour of quiet to answer your welcome letter of the 29 ult. which I received in due time How are you spending these pleasant warm days? I can imagine that most of them find you at the studio making pictures. Well! I haven't delivered any ice yet but expect to begin very soon, tomorrow perhaps. We have just moved into the new barn which we have been building it is quite a nice one being finished upon the inside with planed lumber. Martin was down and stayed over night with me last night and we had an excellent visit he says he likes his school that he is teaching very much Mattie and Edith were in town yesterday but they returned on the train and I did not see them. Father went to Iowa about two weeks ago I think he intends to stay and make it his home but just where or what

business he will go at I don't know and guess he dont either the last I heard from him he was visiting some distant relatives we have there. They have all ready begun paving the streets here, and are intending to have quite a large portion of 2nd 3rd & Main streets. I think it will be a great improvement. You spoke something about my coming to DuBois this summer I would like to very much but it will be impossible for me to get even one day off unless of course it be in case of sickness perhaps it will be a good thing to make me so steady but its hard to think so sometimes. Martie and I were at the Methodist Church this morn but I think perhaps I will attend the Baptist Church this evening. how I wish you were here to go with me but the summer will soon come and go and then if it be His will we may meet again. There was a man died suddenly on the street the other night with heart failure How often such cases come to our notice to remind us of the mortality of mankind Well! I must say good by for this time write soon
from your ever true freind
Norman

Irva sells the majority of his interest in the studio to Phil Griesemer. The celebration of Decoration (Memorial) Day is rained out in Dubois. Curr and Kerr are probably one and the same.

Du Bois, Pa.
May 31st 94
Dear Norman
How do you do to night? I received your very welcome letter some time ago but kept putting off answering it as usual until this late hour. I received a letter from Pa to-day and he said he did wish I would be more prompt in writing but to tell the truth I have been quite busy of late. Well! How does ice delivering go I hope very good I imagine if you are having such weather as we are. It rains here nearly every day. I like where we are living much better than I thought I should who takes care of your Grandmother since your father has gone to Iowa Did he try to get you to go with him. Irva has sold out his interest in the

copying house to his partner Mr Griesemer. I suppose I will work for him just the same at least I like him to work for. Irva thinks he can make more to buy his work. I think I shall get me an air brush next week and then will come the task of learning to use it. Kerr lives out on a farm now and brings his dinner another girl and myself were out there one Sunday we went to the woods and had a great time. The band is playing to-night. I guess they are serenading a newly married couple. Did Jamestown celebrate yesterday? It rained so here that the programming was entirely changed otherwise I guess it would have been good. I am sorry you can't come out this Summer but then such is life. Well! I must close I hope you will excuse this miserable writing my pen is N.G.

Good night

Stella

(write soon)

Celeron Park, the "Coney Island of the West," opened May 18, 1894. The village of Celeron lies at the foot of Chautauqua Lake directly across from Fluvanna and one-and-a-half miles above the boat landing. The Broadhead family, owners of the Jamestown Street Railway, established Celeron as a destination for trolley passengers. In 1893, the rail was laid between the boat landing and Celeron. The line, known as the Chautauqua Traction Co., was soon completed around the west side of the lake to Mayville. Celeron Park operated through the mid-twentieth century. The Fenton Guards were a local militia, mostly ceremonial, named in honor of Reuben E. Fenton, governor of New York 1865-1869, who lived in Jamestown.

Jamestown

June 3

12 M.

Sunday

Dear freind

I received your very kind and welcome letter yesterday. I began to think you had forgotten me entirely. but will now set you a good example by answering promptly; hoping you will do better in this respect in the future. Yes! We have been having very cold rainy weather of late but today it is pleasant and much warmer

and I hope it may continue. I have been delivering ice for 3
weeks now and think I shall like it all right. I have about eighty
customers and will have about twice that number later on I was
up to George's place 3 weeks ago last night and stayed. they are
as well as usual. Howard walks now and goes all around the
farm alone but he doesn't talk a bit and he doesnt need to his sister says enough for both. I have been up to my sisters but once
since I came here The Chaut. Steamboat Co. began two boats
today each of them making two trips around the lake. I think if
warm weather ever comes there will be a very lively season on
the lake this summer. Celeron the place directly across from
Fluvanna is going to be the place this Summer. There has been
many improvements made there among them a toboggan slide a
dance hall and numerous lunch stands etc The place it to be light-
ed by eletricity and there is going to be an electric fountain mod-
eled after the one at the Worlds Fair It did not rain very much
here on May 30 and the exercises were quite good. The street
parade was very good it was made up of Veterans the Fenton
Guards and a number of Lodges. We had the afternoon as a half-
holiday. Do you expect to go home to Sparta this summer for a
vacation. If you do I have been thinking perhaps I might come
out there some Sat. night and back the next night. Goodbye for
this time
Write Soon
Norman

Du Bois, Pa.,
June 16th 1894
Saturday Morning
Friend Norman: –
How do you do? I came down to the studio this morning and
found that Mr Griesemer and Kerr had gone to Falls Creek and
as I don't know of anything much to do will drop you a few
lines. It is very warm here of late – but – it is much nicer than so
much rain I think. We have had several hard thunder storms
here. Have you been on the lake yet? I suppose you don't have
much time though for boat riding. I have been having lots of fun

for the last week or so learning to ride the bicycle. We go over to the fair ground to learn the last night I was there I went clear around the track alone with out stopping. I wish you were going to be here this next week. Monday is aniversary day of the big fire here five or six yrs. ago I guess it was and Thursday & Friday is the land and bicycle tournament I suppose there will be about 20 stands here those days. There will also be races I dont think I will go home before September and maybe not then. I would like to but haven't the time and money to spare. It will be 8 mo. to-morrow since I was home quite a while for a little girl like me isn't it? I have got my air brush but havn't got so I can use it on pictures yet. I suppose it will be some time before I can Mrs. Griesemer is going to Buffalo to visit her sister and wants me to go with her. I would just love to go but guess I cant Do you ever see Mattie I have not heard from her in a long time guess she is paying me back for not writing sooner. I will close for this time hoping to hear from you soon,
Stella.
(Please excuse this paper.)

Sunday Eve.
July 8-94
Dear Stella,
How do you do to night, I have neglected writing to you untill I am almost ashamed to write at all. It is nearly ten o'clock and I have just got home from my brothers where I have been visiting went up on the train at nine this Morning Martie and Mattie were there and also Miss Edith Cobb. I had quite a good time. came back on the Steam-boat. It is quite cool weather here now although we have been having some very warm weather for a few weeks. How did you spend the 4th of July not working I hope. I had to work until about 2 p.m. then I went over town. there I met Martie and was around with him until his train went home about ten p.m. there was quite a crowd here to see the cele-bration which consisted of an industrial Parade, races of various kinds and fireworks, between these amusements a large part of the crowd indulged in "fire water" to such extent that the city lockup was filled to overflowing. Thus passed the glorious

Fourth. Well! It has been a very busy time with us for some time now. The Johnson Ice Co. has 7 teams drawing ice all of the time and some days 8 so you may imagine it takes considerable ice to supply the town I am glad to hear you have learned to ride a bicycle and think it will be healthy exercise for you besides affording you lots of pleasure. I wish I could afford to have one but think I will wait till another season. Have you got so you can use your air brush yet? Write soon and tell me all the news from DuBois also from Sparta and please don't wait so long as I have but write as soon as possible, from your loving freind
Norman

DuBois, Pa.,
Aug 2nd 1894
Dear Friend Norman:
Don't you think I am a good one to correspond with? How are you prospering these days? Can you manage to keep cool with ice around you if so you may consider yourself well off. It has been terrible warm here for the last few weeks. I went to Buffalo with Mrs. Griesemer and had a nice time was at the falls one afternoon. I was gone over a week and came home on the 4th I came home before Mrs. G. did. Jack was there too when we was he went to Chicago and stopped off in Buffalo a week to visit Mrs. G. Eliza has gone to Marionville where Irva is canvassing and so the children and I are alone. They are up to Griesemers to day while I am at the studio. I expect her home Saturday. Is your father in the west yet and what is he working at there. I am writing at the studio. There are some boys up here in the back room playing pedro. I haven't heard from my folks for some time. The last I did they were well as usual maybe I am not home sick to see them I may go home next month and maybe not until Oct. I can't tell I change my mind so often I did not intend going to Buffalo until late the night before I started. Is Martie teaching school yet? Well I must close for this time and go home and get supper. Do not wait forever before answering. Good by.
From your friend,
Stella Murdock.

Allen's Opera House stands on East Second near Main Street. Rebuilt and enlarged after the fire, it remains today the Lucille Ball Little Theater of Jamestown.

Jamestown N.Y.
Aug 9
Thursday eve
Dear freind Stella, –
I received your very welcome letter last Friday and was glad to know you are well. So you have seen Buffalo and Niagara have you? It must have been a very pleasant trip. There is a grand display of fireworks at Celeron to night but I would rather stay at home than go alone so I will improve the opportunity by writing to you. How are you progressing in your work of late? and have you learned to use your air-brush yet? I havent heard from father in a long time I am getting quite anxious about him. When I last heard from him he was visiting relatives at Strawberry Point Iowa. Martin was down and stayed with me last Sat. night. His term of school is out and he is now working at home for the present he is talking seriously of attending the Jamestown Business College this winter but hasn't fully decided yet. Do you ever ride the bicycle anymore? I think it must be very pleasant exercise although I never yet tried it. I took a trip round the lake last Sunday on a Steamboat. Martie was with me as far as Bemus Point on his way home, it is a very pleasant ride. We had a great fire here one week ago tonight Allens Opera House was destroyed by fire caused it is thought by a gas explosion there is nothing left of it but the brick walls As it is nearly bedtime I will draw this poor excuse of a letter to a close I remain as ever your sincere friend
Norman.
"good night"
Write soon.

Forepaugh's, a popular traveling circus, visits Dubois.

DuBois, Pa.
Sept 25 94
Dear friend Norman
I will soon answer your welcome letter which I received so long
ago. I intended to have written long before this but have been
very busy so you must pardon any negligence this time. Are you
still delivering ice? I suppose you will soon be through with that
and find something else to do . Is Martie & Mattie at home now
or are they in the grape country I haven't heard from Mattie or
Rosetta for a long time. Foreparghs show will be here tomorrow
the first thats been here this year. I would like to go but guess I
won't. It is quite cold here to day. My! but I do dread the winter.
You asked if I rode the bycicle much the last time I tried to ride it
I took a tumble and bent the wheel I was on quite badly and so I
haven't tried it since. Irva is away from home as usual, he is gone
nearly all the time. We have a good deal of work in now for Nov.
I would like to go home by the last of next month but don't know
as Mr. Griesemer will think he can spare me. I have to close for
the present.
(Evening)
Well! I commenced this letter this morning and did not finish it
and so I guess I will drop a few more lines and then close Mr.
Griesemers wife & baby have gone visiting to Punxyeutawney to
day will be back to-morrow I guess. How is George's people and
all the rest of your folks? I must close for this time. I hope you
will not wait as long as I did before answering
Good by,
Stella.
Write soon

Norman soon to be out of a job. The season's grape harvest is complete. Ethie Dorne is staying without her sister at the Waterman's. Chauncey Depew, a popular New York politician and respected orator, speaks for the Republicans to a standing room only crowd at the car barns on Third Street.

Jamestown
Nov 4 94
Dear freind Stella
I will now try and answer your welcome letter as I ought to have done long before, although I have neglected writing my thoughts have been with you every day. so when you receive this I hope you will not take revenge on me by waiting as long as I have but write immediately. I am still working for the ice company but this is my last week dont know yet what I shall do this winter because I expected to stay here; until yesterday I was somewhat dissapointed but think I shall find something to do. Two weeks ago today I was up to Watermans visiting it is the first time I had been up that way since last March although Martie was here a couple of times during the summer. Ethie Dorn was there she had been there about a week then She and Mattie worked at the same place in the grape country this fall but I presume you knew this before from Mattie. I heard the other day that Martin had secured a school to teach this winter but have not had a letter from him since I was up there so I don't know for sure about it. Do you hear much about Politics this fall? you would if you were in Jamestown. There was a Mass meeting of between four and five thousand here last Thurs. evening held in the street car barn Chauncey M. Depew was the speaker. Such a meeting as it was makes one think of a presidential campaign rather than a state election I suppose when this reaches you it may be in Sparta but shall direct it DuBois nevertheless. Well as I am getting near the limit of this sheet will close hoping to hear from you very soon. I remain your loving freind
Norman Ingerson
P.S. When you write direct as before 504 West.

Stella's twenty-second birthday. Her letter illustrates Victorian concern and prudence surrounding contagious disease. The Dubois House, a mansion once owned by the town's founder, John Dubois, frequently hosted balls and public events. It is now part of the Penn State University campus at Dubois.

Du Bois, Pa.
Nov 29th 1894.
Dear friend Norman: –
I hardly think you deserve a letter so soon to pay you for not writing before, but nevertheless I will write a few words to let you know I am still living. I had about made up my mind you never were going to write, and if you don't answer this within 6 mo. from now, Well then all right for you. you are quite liable not to get an answer very soon. Well Norman where are you and what are you doing for a living these cold days I have not been home yet but think I will go for Christmas if we are all well by that time. Irva is home, sick with diptheria but is having it in a light form, he is much better to day. I think he will be able to be out again in a few days The children all went down to Mr. Griesemers about as soon as we found out what ailed him so I think they will escape it. There are so many cases of it in town some have died with it. I have been staying at the house to day, was invited out for thanksgiving dinner but thought I hadn't better go for fear I might give the diptheria to some one they say it is so very contageous that one can carry it in their clothes. To day is my birth-day how time flies. How are all of your folks? pa was not very well the last I heard from him I am counting the weeks now until I can go home. Do you think you can come out to Sparta I would like to have you if you can I wonder why Mattie dont answer my letter I have not heard from her for a long time. There is a grand ball at the Du Bois house to-night Jack went; I guess. Well! we have no time for them have we? did you ever see such writeing? I am writeing with Irva's pen and I don't like it a little bit Well good night for this time Write soon and a good long letter. If you can't make this out just take a day off and study it out
Good night
Your friend
S.M.M.

George and Kate's third child, Mary Frances, is born. Kate's sister, Nellie, named after her mother, is probably the young woman also identified as Mattie's cousin.

Bemus Point, N.Y.
(P.O. Box 1213)
Dec. 11-1894
Dear freind Stella, –
How are you tonight, well, I hope. I did not recieve your letter until yesterday as I am now living at Georges and it had been about 2 weeks since I was in Jamestown last. of course I might have had it sent up but expected to go down there sooner than I did. I am sorry to hear that Irva is sick but hope that he is much better by this time and also that you and the rest of his family may escape without being sick. How I wish I knew you were well to night Stella. But! I suppose the only way for us to do is to trust in him who knows what is for the best better than we do. Yes! if nothing happens I will come to Sparta if it is so that you go home. I suppose you will know by the time this reaches you as it is Christmas two weeks from to-day I am afraid your Thanksgiving was rather dull wasn't it considering it was your birthday besides, by the way dont you feel rather old, but then I suppose I've not much to say being only 20 days younger. I had a letter from father the other day he is well and seems to like it quite well where he is. he said mercury had been down to zero once or twice. That is somewhat colder than we have had isn't it. Georges folks have a girl baby about six weeks old its name is Mary Frances. Kate's sister Nellie is working here. I went up to my Aunts last Sunday the one where Pa was a year ago. Mildred went with me she is getting to be quite a large girl most 4 years old she says. I havent seen any of Waterman's people since I wrote you before. Martie has been teaching a little this fall he fin- ished a term for another teacher but what he is doing since I don't know. Mattie has been to visit Ethie so I hear. she got back about two weeks ago. I didn't tell you how my grandmother is. she keeps just about as she was a year ago. I wonder how long she can live in this way. well as I have pretty nearly covered this sheet of paper and it is getting late I will say good night. You

must write as soon as you get this for I am very anxious to know that you havent caught the diptheria.
goodby for this time
Norman

Stella returns to Sparta for Christmas.

Spartansburg, Pa.
Dec 22
Friend Norman
I thought I would write you a few lines to day. I came to Spartansburg last Thursday. Lulu came with me. Irva was working again when I came away and all the rest of the family were well. I am going to the burg to day I guess Write and let me know when you will be out - Can you come for New Years. Well I haven't much time to write so please excuse this short letter and write soon.
Good by
From you friend Stella.

Bemus Point N.Y.
Dec. 26, 1894
Freind Stella
I received your welcome letter yesterday was very glad to hear you were well and enjoying a visit home. Well if nothing happens I will be down to Sparta next Monday Dec. 31. I do not know what time the train goes but I will start in the morning sometime. My sister's people were here yesterday we had a very nice time there are a great many things I would like to say but havent time as George is going to the Point and I must close so as to send the letter I am writing by him.
good by excuse this short letter.
Norman

Monday. Written at Bemus Point two days after Norman's return. Norman spent twelve days with Stella in Sparta. Despite no longer working for Mr. Johnson, he stayed two nights at the Johnson property in Jamestown before returning to George's dairy farm. The Erie Railroad track skirts the lower end of Chautauqua Lake near Lakewood and Celeron.

Bemus Point
Jan 14-95
Dear Freind Stella –
I wonder what you are doing this afternoon. Enjoying yourself I suppose at least I hope so. I arrived in Jamestown at about 15 min after 4 o'clock Sat. afternoon. had to wait nearly an hour in Corry. I stayed at Mr. Johnson's till this morning. My people are all as well as usual. Mildred and Howard are sitting near me talking a steady stream; but then you know I am not nervous so it doesn't make any difference with my writing. George is at the barn working and Kate is washing. I am going to the P.O. toward Eve so I think perhaps you will receive this epistle while at home 'twould be a terrible thing if you didn't, wouldn't it? It has been quite cold here since Sat. evening with a fall of about six inches of snow and still it snows. so you see we have good sleighing here again. I suppose it is sleighing down your way too and hope you may be able to improve it this week. George has been trading horses since I went away so I shall drive a new team this afternoon. I have not decided as to what I shall do in regard to the milk business. but I am to meet a man "who is agent for machinery such as we need" in town next Saturday and make arrangements if possible to buy our stock new and start in independently of the other company which I think is a better way. Did you get home all right and without getting run away with Saturday? There was a great crowd of people skating at Celeron when I came past on the train Sat at least a Thousand so they said. I hope that you may learn this winter. then when I come to see you next winter we'll have a picnic wont we though. Well I must draw this to a close and go out and help George enough to pay for my board. I hope when I write again I may be able to say I am making more than my board or at least have some prospects of doing so some time I hope you will answer as soon as you get

this and that it will find you and all the rest of my freinds well.
good by for this time
with more than freindship
Norman
(s.w.a.k.)

IV

unless something happens

The tone of the 1895 letters and their expressions of love and affection in closing indicate that Norman and Stella are now truly committed to each other. Norman's visit on the new year must have confirmed that commitment. The courtship by mail has continued for more than two years. During that time the two have seen each other on only three occasions. The rather formal Victorian quality of their visits to each other's home is often referenced in their letters. Yet, despite the formality and the separation, the courtship has matured.

Norman's new position at the Jamestown Cotton Mill is his first non-seasonal employment and carries with it a responsibility commensurate with his image of himself. He joins several, mostly church-related organizations appropriate to his emergence into Victorian respectability. His wages are increasing and his prospects bright.

Stella finds solace and social contact through the church at Dubois. Although she is often lonely and homesick, she decides she really does prefer the "advantages" of urban life over the isolation of Sparta. She has never felt appreciated, nor does she seem to enjoy the work at the studio. A personality conflict with her employer, Phil Griesemer, results in her return, with hurt feelings, to Sparta. Norman, now confident in himself and his future, visits her there and proposes.

Stella and Lulu spend the night with Spartansburg friends Edna and Evart Frost. John Griesemer has left the studio. A sleigh ride vividly described. Lizzie Pierce is probably Eliza's sister and Bell Shreave, a friend.

DuBois, Pa.
Jan 28th 1895
Dear Norman:

I received your very welcome letter a week ago last wednesday and intended answering it before but have been very busy since I came back. We came Saturday after you left as we intended, stayed at Evarts the night before. Well I have been here a little over a week and it seems more like two. John is not working at the studio any more and so I have been framing pictures some this last week. I suppose you know what you are going to do about the dairy business by this time It has been very cold here for the last few days and stormy too. There were two loads went from here to Penfield (about 13 miles) for a sleigh ride last wednesday night. Irva and Eliza went and so I went with them and such a time as we had you can't imagine. it was colder I think than when we came from Union and we got into the awfulest drifts the boys got out and broke down fences to go through the fields and tramped snow so we could get through we started from here about seven or a little after and never reached there until about twelve taking us about five hours to drive a distance we aught to have driven in two. I think I never suffered so with the cold in my life. Well when we got to Penfield the boys routed out the hotel keeper and we went in and got warm and had a cup of coffee and then some of them rented a hall right near the hotel and danced until about four and then we came home again we were not near as long coming home but I don't ever want to take another such sleigh ride, I went to church last evening there are protracted meetings being held here now. Bell Shreave & Lizzie Pierce were up to see me after you went away don't you wish you had been there. Norman you can't imagine how I hated to leave my folks again. I sometimes wish I had never seen Du Bois. if it wasn't so far away and I could go home oftener I would not care so much but I don't think I will ever stay away from home as long as I have again. Irvas folks have all gone to bed and I must quit writing and go too. I hope you will answer soon.
Good Night, from your ever true friend.
Stella.
S.W.A.K.

Driftwood is a lake shore neighborhood near Fluvanna. Norman's mother, Cornelia Haskin Ingerson, is mentioned for the first time. His expression "didn't have much of a time" signifies the opposite.

Bemus Point N.Y.
Feb 10, 1895
Thurs. Eve.
Dear Stella, –
How do you get along this cold weather? I received your most welcome letter last Saturday. I worked on the ice at Driftwood last week every day and boarded with the folks that live in the house where we used to It did not seem like home at all in fact it was hard to make it seem as though I had ever lived there at all, things are changed so. My! but we've been having some cold weather lately. night before last mercury dropped to 18 below 0 and it scarcely gets above the cipher during the day. George is filling his ice house this week. We have to draw it over 2 miles Yes! I know what I am going to do about the Dairy business. We are going to start in new We have secured a location on third st. 2 squares from the P.O. our machinery we expect will come about Mar. 1st and we hope to get started about the middle or last of the month Kate says you better give up the portrait business and come out and work for her this summer. wouldn't that be nice though. Mother is here for a few days and also one of Kate's uncles and his wife and child. It makes me feel as though I ought to be somewhere else and make the crowd one smaller. I wish I knew I would be successful this summer sometimes I wish I had never tried to start in the business for if I should make a failure I would be worse off than I am now. but I hope for the best Kate and Nellie and I were to a party at Mr. Cothrells the other night and didn't have much of a time either. Well Stella have you been homesick any more lately? I hope not at least have you had any sleigh rides since you went to Penfield It has been fine sleighing here ever since I came home How I wish you were here wouldn't we enjoy some of it though. I must close for this time as it is nearly nine o'clock and you know I'm a great hand to go to bed early. hoping to hear from you very soon I remain as ever your loving freind
Norman

DuBois, Pa.,
Feb 13 1895
Dear Norman
Your very welcome letter at hand. Don't let the surprise of receiving an answer so soon make you sick. I have been very busy ever
since I came back until within the last few days haven't had
much to do but practiceing Don't it keep you hustleing to keep
warm these cold days. Last friday was a terrible day here. I have
been to church quite a good deal since I came back. We are having splendid meetings here now. Eliza has joined the church on
probation. She says she was converted at home. Well! I hope you
may be successful in the dairy business. I haven't been skating
since I came back and don't think I will this winter. No I haven't
been a sleighriding since we went to Penfield nor I havnt been
hardly any place except to church and I have made up my mind
to never dance again. Well I will have to close I guess for this
time as it is supper time and I can't think of anything interesting
to you to write.
So good by
write very soon from
Your loving friend
Stella
(Excuse this paper)

*References to dancing in this and the previous letter imply that Norman and
Stella attended a dance together during Norman's recent visit.*

Bemus Point
Feb 24. 1895
Dear Stella, –
I received your very welcome letter one week ago yesterday and
meant to have answered it before this. Well Stella how do you get
along this cold weather. Mercy! did you ever see it as cold before.
The C. L. Ry. has been Blockaded since last Thurs but I think will
be open tomorrow This has been a lovely day just right for a
sleighride dont you wish we could take Coaly and have a little
drive this Eve. The snow is so deep in places that we have to

drive though fields and dooryards or any where to get around
the drifts. I intend to drive to Jamestown to morrow if nothing
happens I havent been to church very much lately not as much as
I ought to have been. but I havent been to any dances either and,
well! I dont think I will go to any very soon I dont feel very
proud of the fact that I did go How is it with you? I was glad to
hear that your sister-in-law has joined the church and only wish
there were more like her. What did she mean by saying she was
converted at home? I think I know but not for sure How do your
father and Dot get along. I think They must be stormed in most
of the time dont you? I cant think of much of interest to write so I
hope you will excuse a short letter this time and write very very
soon to your loving freind
Norman
(s.w.a.k.)

Sparta
March 24 1895
Dear Stella
I know you will be looking for a letter before this I hav tride to
git time to write but could not I thought I could write to day but
hav bin so bissey I could not I hav not got enney help yet but will
have a boy hand one weak from to day I sopose. he is small for
his age he is 19 years old Has Mr Grismer got work for you yet if
you cant find work dont go and get married but come home I
will keep you so dont worrey Stella I think perhaps your tring to
be a better christen a good thing if Mr Grismer on the account of
that did not want you it is all rite I hope the man you spoke of
will find you a place whar you will not hav to hear so much that
I know dont sute you. I am glad Elisa has joined the church I
think a christian mother can rais those dear children better Will
and Roze was her one weak ago to day they had Little Frank
with them he is verry nice for all of his name O Stella I have got
me one of the nises littel puppes you ever saw he is nerly white
how I wish you was hear to sea him and to eat warm sugar with

us this spring I will hav to stop riting for this time I am fealing
better only I git so tired you must excuse this led pensel for the
ink is so far I could not use it so god by and write sone
Love to all
Frank

Stella's troubles with Phil Griesemer have begun. Pa reacts. The importance of
church in Stella's life is clearly indicated. The mother of Charlie Parker and
Edna Parker Frost dies.

Du Bois, Pa.
April 1st '95
Dear Friend Norman: –
Your letter received a long time ago and meant to have surely
answered it before this but you know it is nothing new for me to
neglect writing and I suppose there is no use of making excuses.
Have you started in the Dairy business yet? I havn't had only
three weeks work since I came back and guess I won't work for
Phil any more. don't think he will want me any more. I have sold
my air brush and may get a place in some store here to clerk I
will know in a few weeks I guess. If I cant' get anything to do
that suits me I will go home. We are having Union Evangelistic
meeting here and they are something grand the Evangelist Mr
Schiverea is the best speaker I think I ever heard last evening
there was a meeting for lady's only at the church at 7 and at 8
oclock in the opera house for men only and the seats were full
and women standing around the doors and aisles it was in the
M.E. Church last evening because it is larger than other churches
and they have meetings in other churches for those that cant get
in. Yesterday I went to 5 oclock prayer meeting church at half
past 9 and at 11 then sunday school and church again at 7 There
were more I think at 6 o'clock prayer meeting before daylight
than at 11 oclock preaching. I just wish you could hear him. It is
raining here today. I wish you was here I wouldn't play cards as
we did when I was home but I guess we would find something
to do. I have changed my mind somewhat concerning card playing This evangelist thats here has a good deal to say against cards
& dancing Had you heard that Charlie Parkers mother is dead.

She was at Ednas when she died. I am so sorry now that I did not go to see her while I was home. I did just run in a little while that evening you remember. How is Mattie & Martie I guess Mat has entirely forgotten me. This is April fool and the children are trying to fool some of us. Irva is having a summer kitchen built and of all the pounding. Well dinner is ready and so I will close for this time now please dont wait a month before writing
Good by
Stella
S.W.A.K.

Eugene and Nora were married shortly after the 1892 grape harvest (letters Nov. 17 and Dec. 4, 1892).

Dewittville N.Y.
Apr 21 1895
Dear Stella,
I received your letter but a few days ago I was glad to hear that you were well as I had about made up my mind that you was sick. You must never write another letter on April 1st. I never got this till the 17 I think it was. I wonder if you will be surprised to know that I didn't go in to that business as I intended. We were nearly ready to start but when Hotchkiss tried to get his money he found he could not get it so we dropped it. I am now working for Norman Waterman Mattie's uncle Who owns a cheese factory. It is about two miles from Dewittville. I don't know as yet whether I shall stay all summer or not. It seems strange to think you are not working in the Studio any more. I hope you will find something that suits you. but someway it seems as though you might do worse than to stay at home for a while anyway. There are revival services at Dewittville now a Mr. Barret & his wife are conducting them I have been a number of times and enjoy them very much. Oh! how slow it is to write what one wants to say here I've nearly filled this sheet and havent said anything either. Martie is teaching school and Mattie is at home she has hired out at Chaut. to work during the assembly. Kate's sister Nellie Reardon has the Malarial fever I think that is what they call it.

I was at Denton's corners to church this Afternoon Mattie and Fred Smith were there also Eugene and Nora by the way they (Eugene & Nora) live quite near here. Well I must draw this to a close as supper is nearly ready. now Stella don't wait before you answer this as I am anxious to know what you are going to do. good by for this time
with love
Norman

Stella does wait. Spring cleaning is her excuse for not having written sooner.

Du Bois, Pa.
May 25th 95
Dear Norman: –
Is it possible that it has been a month since I rec'd your very welcome letter? Well I looked in vain for it for a long time and as I have been very busy helping Eliza clean house you must pardon me this time. yes I was quite surprised to hear that you did not go into the business you intended to are you still at Mr. Watermans? You said he owned a cheese factory you work in it I suppose. I am still rather undecided about what I am going to do I may go home next week and I may stay here all summer. I think though that I will go home. I don't like the idea of leaving Du Bois very well either. I didn't used to care much for the place but since I have become better accquainted I like it here better. I will miss the advantages I have of going to church greatly if I do go home. We have been having heavy frosts here and also out home. do you ever see Mattie & Martie Oh! yes you wrote about them in your letter. Is Marts cousin at their house yet Lulu is taking music lessons this summer she and some other little girls have taken a lunch and gone to the woods this afternoon. It is supper time and so I will bring this to a close I hope you will answer as soon as you get this but I will be quite surprised if you do I see I have written quite a long letter and nothing much in it either
Good by for this time yours
with love, Stella.

The Jamestown Cotton Mill was located on Harrison Street in east Jamestown. The Erie Railroad track is just north. The mill was owned by Thomas Henry Smith and made cotton batting to stuff comforters. Norman's new boarding house at 108 Crescent Street is within easy walking distance. He is clearly delighted with his new position for which Jamestown Business College has qualified him. Norman is confused over Stella's whereabouts at the beginning of the letter because he understands that she is no longer working at the studio.

Jamestown N.Y.
Direct, 108 Crescent St
June 6-1895
Dear Stella,
I read your very welcome letter today and will try and surprise you by answering it immediately. It must have been delayed at Dewittville a long time as I see you wrote it May 25, No! I am not at Mr. Watermans any more I have been here in town four weeks next Monday. I am keeping Books for the Jamestown Cotton Mill and I think I shall like it very much, after I get a little more used to it. As I write I wonder what you are doing tonight I can hardly make it seem as though you could be at Your Fathers after being so long at DuBois. Well! if you are at home I hope you wont be lonesome. The Place where I work is quite near the Railroad and that with the many other noises makes it quite interesting. There are about 60 hands in the Factory and I am the only Bookkeeper so you see I am kept pretty busy most of the time. I have to attend to the shipping and I am also Paymaster. We pay every two weeks and the wages amount to nearly $700 for two weeks as we pay with cash instead of Checks as a great many such places do I have to handle quite a bit of money. I enjoy going to Church here very much we have very good services in all of the Churches but of course I go to the Baptist as a rule, I am writing at the office in the factory and the Electric Light has been turned off so that there is nothing left to see by but an old gas lamp so let's say
Good night and I will finish this in the Morning.
Friday June 7,
 7 A.M.
I will now try and finish this so that the Postman can take it when he comes. I did not tell what wages I am getting I have to

start in quite cheap but hope to get more after a while At first I had $7 per week but am getting $7.50 now. I have a nice place to board they are Christian people I am glad for that. We have very sudden changes in the weather this summer dont we. If I could be with you Stella I believe I could tell you so much that I cant express on paper but I suppose it is not right for it to be that way or it would be, I was at George's 2 weeks ago Sunday. They are all well. Kate's Birthday is to day I believe she said They are going to be at her Mothers at Mayville next Sunday and wanted me to be up there too. don't know whether I shall go or not as I have lots to do to day well, say good by for this time
your loving friend
Norman

Jamestown Cotton Mill, looking over the Erie Railroad tracks.

Eliza's sister, Gertie, may be Mrs. Gertie Goldstein, who worked the grape harvest in 1892 (letters Nov. 7, 1892; June 6, 1893).

Du Bois
July 10th 1895.
Wednesday Evening
Dear Norman: –
Do you think I am never going to answer your letter? I do feel rather ashamed for being so negligent but will try and do better next time. I am still in Du Bois think now that I may be here for some time yet, have been working at the studio for over a month now. I thought when I wrote you last that I would be home by this time But there has been so much work in the studio of late that I have been kept pretty busy here. I am glad to hear of your new position hope you will continue to like it I suppose you do not have much time to yourself do you? Wish you could come out. What did you do the 4th I went to the bicycle races at the fair ground here. There were a good many people in town but was not much going on that was very interesting to me. Will is here now he is working for Phil and Irva, he has just brought me a letter from home. Pa is working very hard this summer as usual. Lulu & Mate have gone to a taffy pull this evening at one of our neighbors. Gertie (Elizas sister) & husband were here the 4th came on wednesday and stayed until Saturday. Do you board with the man you are working for or do you have to board yourself? Well! I wish I could see you it seems like a long while since I was home. I get dreadfully homesick sometimes but that is all the good it does me. I wish that Irva's folks lived nearer home I could go home oftener then. I must close for this time as it is getting late I hope you will be as prompt in answering this as you was before. I received quite a calling down from Pa & Dot in their letter for not writing oftener so you see you are not the only one that I neglect writing to.
Good night,
from your friend Stella.

Martie Waterman marries his cousin Edith Cobb. Norman purchases his wheel.

Jamestown, N.Y.
July 20
Sat. Afternoon at 4 P.M.
Dear Stella, –
I received your very welcome letter a week since and will now
try and answer it, how do you get along these hot days for I suppose it is hot in DuBois same as here. Had you heard that Martie
was married to Edith Cobb it happened about three weeks ago. I
am sorry and thats all I have to say about it. He was down and
stayed with me over night one week ago yesterday. I was somewhat surprized to find you did not go home. I was in hopes you
would go home and I intended coming down some Sat afternoon
and Stay over Sunday I can't get away any other time as I know
of I am kept very busy I can tell you everything being new to me
but I am becoming more expert every day so the work comes easier for me I worked on the Books all day the fourth of July and
every evening also for a week or two but am getting along better
now. Oh! I wish I could Just be with you this afternoon Stella. I
have so much to say and the pen is such a poor thing to say it
with but I am trying to be contented and wait. I have bought me
a Bicycle and I think I shall go up to Georges on it to night! have
you ever rode any since last summer? I think its great sport. I got
a fall when I was learning a week ago to day and had to go
around all this week with my face scratched up. Wouldn't you
like my picture though. I suppose Mattie is working at Chaut.
this summer. the season there is very busy they say I wish you
could be up here and go one or two days. I have not been anywhere much since I began here and don't suppose I will go very
much. No! I do not board with Mr. Smith but I have a very good
place with a private family Williams by name. Please do not wait
before answering this but write immediately if you knew how I
look for a letter and think maybe you are sick or something you
wouldn't wait so long again Good bye for this time
With Love
Norman

July 31st 1895

Dear Friend Norman:

Yours of a few day ago at hand and as I am not very busy now will improve the time by dropping you a few lines. It is now about 9 A.M. and I am at the studio so will use this paper this time if you will excuse it. Mr. Griesemer has gone to Buffalo on an excursion and so Kerr, Jack & myself are manageing things for the present. I would like to have went to the Falls but that was rather out of the question this time. There is also an excursion from here to Chautauqua Saturday the 3rd Eliza intends going and then going out home by going that way she can spend a day at the lake all for about the same price. So if you want to see her you can meet her at the depot. I think the train will reach there about 10 or 11 at Jamestown, I was quite surprised to hear that Martie is married are they at his folk's yet? I have had the tooth ache most of the time now for nearly a week It is one I had filled a short time ago and it has bothered me ever since. I am most afraid I will have to have it out yet. Sunday was old peoples meeting here. Services conducted something like they were fifty years ago sang without an organ or choir etc. I was to near crazy with my tooth to go in the morning but went in the evening. Yes I would like one of your photos but be sure you can manage the bicycle before you attempt having them taken. Have you taken any more falls lately? We are having quite cool weather here now which is quite welcome after so much heat. You will have to bear with a short letter this time for I can't think of anything worth writing wish I was going to Chautauqua with Eliza and you could go to. I am rather anxious to go home but guess I will wait a while yet unless some of the folks get sick. Father is very poorly this summer he will work though whether he is able to or not.

Well Good by

write soon,

Stella.

Governor of Ohio and future Republican President William McKinley visits Chautauqua. McKinley spoke briefly the previous evening at the annual campfire and at length the afternoon this letter was written, Grand Army Day.

Jamestown, N.Y.

August 24 – 1895

Dear Freind Stella,

Your welcome letter received some time ago How are you getting along These hot days I suppose you are still working for Mr. Griesemer. I am still at The Cotton Mill and like it first rate. I do not have to work near as hard as I am getting more accustomed to it Do you hear from home very often? I suppose you will soon be going there for a visit wont you? I was up to Mr. A.L. Watermans a week ago to day rode my wheel up and came back the next night Martin is there at present but expects to begin teaching one week from Next Monday. It is a quite large school about 5 miles East of Jamestown There are 2 Departments he is to teach one and his wife the other. he gets $10 and she 7 I think they are very fortunate On the Evening of the 15th there was an Illuminated fleet at Chaut. A Party of 16 from our Young Peoples Society chartered a small Steamer and went we had a very nice time I wish you might have seen it it was a very pretty sight I have Joined the Y.M.C.A. at last. This gives me a great many privileges among them is the Free use of the bath rooms. I suppose that Wm McKinley of Ohio is at Chaut. to day I would like to hear him speak but could not get away. Did Mrs. Murdock come through Jamestown as you spoke of. I could not get up to the train that day as it was Payday and at the time the train came I was right in the midst of it. Well I have written all I can think of that will interest you so will close hoping to hear from you soon, Norman

Irva's studio identified. Stella's letter reveals the scope of the American Artists Alliance.

Du Bois, Pa.
Sept 16th 1895
Dear Norman: –
With pleasure I now take pen in hand to answer your very welcome letter of a few weeks ago. Well Norman how are you getting along? I thought you were a good while answering my last letter didn't know you were never going to write again. Is it cold enough for you now? We had quite a heavy frost Saturday night, which reminds one that winter is not far away. I am still working at the studio my work is mostly writing now. Business has greatly improved with the American Artists Alliance We have had more work on hand and will have up till Christmas than ever before in fact there has been such an increase in work that it has become necessary for Mr. Griesemer to rent more rooms Just across the street from where we now are he has five rooms for storeing some of the frames and Kerr & Jack also work over there which gives us quite a space to what we did have. Mr. G's youngest brother from Chicago is here now he works in the shipping room so there is five of us kept busy here besides about 12 to 15 agents on the road. I am glad you have joined the Y.M.C.A. It seems to be quite a strong order or association here. I wish I might have seen the Illuminated fleet you speak of. Mrs. M. was quite dissapointed at not seeing you the day she went through Jamestown, she missed the train there and did not reach Sparta until after 12 that night she was gone three weeks and a long three weeks it was to me. I would like so much to go home while it is pleasant weather but guess I will have to be contented for a long while yet. I have not heard from home for a long while am quite worried I thought sure I would get a letter to day Is Mattie picking grapes this fall? I hear that Mr. Dorn (Ethies father) has lost his mind that was several weeks ago havn't heard from him lately he may be all right by this time. To-morrow is Lulu's birthday she will be 13 years old she is going to have a party in the evening she has invited about 25 I guess won't we have music though? Norman I wish you might come out I would like so

much to see you come some Sat. and stay over Sunday or longer
if you can Can't you? Eliza has gone down town and the children
are to bed and I am alone Our minister went to conference and I
hear is sent on another charge. I am so sorry for I liked him so
well. Do you attend Sunday school? Well Eliza has got back and
as it is getting rather late guess I will draw this to a close for this
time. I hope to receive an answer sooner than before. Write all the
news and a good long letter. How is your brothers people
remember me to them
Good by,
From you affectionate friend
Stella.
S.W.A.K.

*Death of Grandmother Susan Waterman Ingerson. Norman's father returns
from Iowa.*

Jamestown,
Sept 19-95
Dear Stella,
I recd your letter yesterday. I had begun to think that you was
trying to see if you could wait longer than I did before writing,
but I am going to surpize you pleasantly, I hope; by answering
promptly, Well! I am still at the same place as when I wrote you
before I like it first rate. I am very busy all of the time The only
fault I have to find is with my wages. It is now over four months
since I began here and I think I am worth more than 7 1/2 a week
but I suppose I must be patient. Grandma Ingerson died Last
Sunday. The funeral was Tuesday. This is the first day I have been
away from my work since I began. Father came home just in time
for the funeral. I sent him a telegram Sunday but he had started
before and did not know of Grandmother's death untill he
reached Dewittville, Maybe you think I wasnt glad to see him
Georges people are all well I was there visiting last Sunday They
have three pretty cute little ones. I think. Yes! Mattie is picking
grapes this fall I dont know the people where she works, but
think it is the same place where she worked last fall. Martie is
teaching school about 5 miles from here at a little place called

Levant. It is a school of two departments and he teaches one room and his wife the other. He receives $10 and she $7 per week. they have rented rooms and are keeping house I was there once or twice. It seems funny or queer rather to think of Martie as married I only hope (now that it is over with and cannot be helped) that he will never have cause to regret it. I am sorry to hear you can't go home for so long I really dont think its right for you to stay away so long just as though you had to work every day in order to live. Well! I wish I could be with you to night Stella It makes me almost homesick to think how little prospect there is of my coming to visit you I had thought when you went home I could easily come down there but it seems as though Du Bois is 1000 miles away. but then if I have my health Stella I shall come and see you in less than six mo's if I have to lose my position. Mr Smith My employer has a son about my age who understands the work in the office quite well and I perhaps can get him to take my place for a few days after the rush of the season is over But now see here I think you might take a vacation and come up this way and see the Lake and people My brothers wife asks me about you nearly every time I go up there and says she thinks you might come up visiting Yes! I go to Sunday School when I am in town on Sunday. I am getting quite well acquainted with a number of the young people in the church here I also belong to the Baptist Young Peoples Union Stella you dont know how thankful I am that I was a Christian before I came to this place its an easy matter to get in good company and do whats right if one only starts right but I think it would be more easy to go wrong. There has been no regular pastor for our church during the summer. but on Oct 1st Dr. Adams of Franklin Pa. takes the pulpit for one year at least. I think I shall like him he is a very eloquent man and seems thoroughly in earnest. I dont think you can find any fault but that this is a long enough letter. now when you get this I hope you will take time to answer it very soon It is nearly nine and I always make a practise of going to bed early as you know. so I will close for this time
Good night
with love
Norman

Du Bois,
Sept 27 1895
Dear Norman:
Yours of the 19th received. I was some what surprised at your
promptness in answering what is going to happen any way? I havn't
much room to talk in that line I guess you will think so will drop the
question. Can you manage to keep warm these days? only to think
that it is allmost winter again. Irva is at home now guess he will be at
home more than he has been I hope so at least. I hear that Ethie's &
Nora's father is dead was buried last Saturday poor girls how hard
they will take it. They allways seemed to think so much of their parents. Lulu has been out riding on Irva's wheel she can go pretty good
she can only reach the peddles when they come up. Do you ever see
Rosetta I wonder what she thought about Martie getting married. I
think he and his wife are very lucky at getting such a good position
some better than picking grapes isn't it? I believe I would enjoy being
in the grape country again, for a little while at least. Remember the
day we picked grapes and it snowed wasn't that terrible. I havn't got
a letter from home yet was quite worried until I got a letter from
Rose the other day stateing they were all well. Is your father going
back west again how strange that he happened to come home just in
time for his mothers funeral without knowing of her death. I would
like very much to go home and stop at the lake but guess that will be
quiet impossible. I am quite uncertain when I can go home you say
you get $7.50 per week how much do you have to pay for board I
think you ought to get more too but suppose you will after while if
you are patient I think I ought to get more than 3 a week but Mr. G.
don't seem to think so Irva would be willing to pay me more if he
would but that is better than earning nothing. I was to hear our new
preacher Sunday. I like him very much. I wish Norman I might talk
to you instead of writing but will have to be contented I suppose at
writing. Well I have scribbled this sheet nearly full and haven't written much either don't know whether you can read it or not for the
mistakes. I wrote it in such a hurry
Good night for this time and
write soon
lovingly yours
Stella

Murdock Family, Ca. 1902.
First Row: Stella, Mate, Merrill Plyler (Lulu's husband)
Middle Row: Rilla, Lulu
Standing: Eliza, Norman Ingerson, Will, Irva

Jamestown
Oct. 21-95
Dear Stella,

 I am almost ashamed to write I have neglected it so long, but if you will pardon me this time I will try and do better in the future. How do you stand it this cold weather, We have been having a regular winter here since Sat. I rode my wheel up to my sisters Saturday afternoon and when I got up the next morning the ground was white with snow and the air was full of it. Just like a winter blizzard for all the world but I had to leave my bicycle and come home on the train. I have not been up to Georges since Grandma's funeral, George and Kate were down town a week or so ago and I went up to the hotel and ate dinner with them. I am still working at the same place I like the work first rate and think if all goes well will get something for it someday. I am now getting $8 per week I have to pay $3.50 for board so you see I have just $18 per Mo. or rather for four weeks. I have $18 left after paying my board. I think with the prospect of getting more in the near future it is a good bit better than working on a farm. No! I don't ever see Rosetta When I was working at Watermans last Spring I saw her a few times but someway didn't have much of a visit with her Do you know yet when you are going home? I suppose the Artists Alliance is in its busiest season now. I would like ever so much to come to Du Bois but don't like to ask for a vacation and really I don't see how they can spare me we are very busy all of the time. Mr. Smith the Prop. has gone to Atlanta Ga., for a week or two and It leaves the business with his son (who is a year or two younger than I) and myself. by the way what do you do since you sold your airbrush. have you bought it back or not. No Father is not going back west not right away at least he is now staying at my Aunts where Grandmother lived. I enjoy the advantages of being where I can attend church regularly I have taken my letter from the church at Dentons and united with this one. We have had no regular Pastor in the Baptist church during the summer but will have after the first Sunday in November Rev. Dr. Adams, formerly of Franklin Pa. is the man We have a very nice Sunday School and a Young Peoples Society which meets Sunday evenings one hour before Preaching service There

is also a Bible study class which meets every Friday evening. Two weeks ago last Sat. I attended a Y.M.C.A. convention at Dunkirk lasting over Sunday there was 6 or seven of us from this place I enjoyed it very much. Well! I think if I did wait quite a while before writing I have made this long and tedious enough to make up. Now please don't follow my example but write soon and, Good night for this time
Lovingly
Norman
SWAK

From Eliza Murdock. Cecil is the hired man at Pa's farm.

DuBois, Pa.
Oct 30, 1895
Dear Sister Stella
Your letter recd which finds us all well only Mate has a bad cold Irva is away we went on his delivery Monday I am sorry you are discontented but I would not know what to tell you Irva will be gone about 2 weeks I expect. I told Phill I guessed you would like to come back he did not make much of a reply only he said he did not know what ailed you he said after you went around awhile without speaking he got up on his dignity and you got so you did not like to be critisised, but did not think it advisable for you to come back. Phill moved yesterday on Olive st, it is a pleasant place I take care of Freida for them Phill and Johnny came in Wednesday of last week and went to Ridgway Monday They did not make a very long stay in Maryland Mama sent her wheel here and told us we might learn to ride so we think we will soon be experts I want to attend the conference meeting this afternoon they say it is very interesting I will send you the program I would like to have your Pa and Dot come out coax them to come out they have no excuse for you and Cecil can look after things for them, Irva forwarded a letter from Jamestown to you did you get it I want you to visit at our place and let me know how they are well I guess I have wrote all the news I can think of good by love to all
Eliza

Stella leaves Dubois for good. Her September 27, 1895, letter gave no indica-
tion she was planning to leave. Norman's October 21, 1895, letter reaches her
in Sparta three weeks after her arrival. Further problems with Phil provoked
her departure. She writes from her father's house lonely, depressed and wishing
to see Norman.

Spartansburg, Pa.
Nov. 1st 95.
Dear friend Norman: –
Your letter recd a few days ago and found me in Sparta which I
suppose you will be rather surprised to hear from what I wrote
you before. I came home three weeks ago tomorrow left DuBois
three weeks ago yesterday stopped off in Youngsvill and made
my cousin there a visit and came on out home the next Saturday.
I found Pa in town he was quite surprised to see me as he did not
know I was coming. I do not expect to go back to DuBois again to
work. I am dreadfully lonesome some of the time since I came
back I like living in town the best Pa is feeling very poorly and it
isn't much wonder for he is working so very hard. When do you
think you can come out? Can't you come some Sat. night and
stay at least over Sunday. We are having very cold weather I
think for this time of year. I am glad you have an increase in
wages hope you may still get more. Well I will close for I don't
know of anything worth writing. I shall look for you out a week
from to-morrow let me know if you can come. Good by for this
time and write soon,
Your friend Stella.

Jamestown
Nov 7-95
Dear Stella,
I recd your very welcome letter day before yesterday am very
busy. I am just back from dinner and will steal a few minutes for
you Yes! I was very much surprized that you had gone home so
soon. You did not write any thing about why you did not stay
longer in DuBois. I am still at the same place as when I wrote you
before. Aren't we having warm weather though for November. I
am sorry to say I can't come down to see you next Sat. but think

if nothing happens I will come a week from Sat. Nov. 16. This is the week that we pay so that I shall have to be here I suppose. I attended a concert last Monday Eve in the M.E. Church which was very fine I wish you might have heard it. It was the opening Entertainment in the Epworth League Lecture Course The Y.M.C.A. has a lecture Course also which my membership admits me to I am going to one tonight a lecture by Russel H. Conwell did you ever hear him I never did, but those who have say he is very fine. Next week is the week of Prayer for Young Men in The Y.M.C.A. It consists of a bible study every Afternoon and an Evangelistic service evenings. The evening services are going to be led by the Pastors of the different churches. Well! I shall have to close for this time as I have so much to do and will save the rest of the news till I can come down.

Good by for this time

Yours with love

Norman

(Write soon)

Excuse this envelope

Jamestown N.Y.

Nov. 11 1895

Dear Stella,

If nothing happens to hinder I will come down next Friday Nov. 15 Will leave here on the train at 7-45 A.M. and it makes close connection at Corry so that I will get to Sparta about 10 oclock probably, I am very thankful that it is possible for me to come before Sat afternoon for I will have to come back early Monday Morn. as I am very, very Busy this morning will say good bye,

Hastily yours

Norman

Victorian fatalism clearly expressed. Norman writes alone in his room to his sad and lonely beloved just after having proposed.

Jamestown N.Y.
Nov 19-1895
Dear Stella, –
I arrived safely yesterday got here about 10 o'clock. I have been quite busy since I got back but my work is not behind a great deal in fact I can hardly see any difference. What time did you get back home I suppose you went over to Will's a while did you not It is raining this evening. It has been so warm and pleasant all day though that one most forgets that winter is so near. I don't dread winter very much as I feel quite sure that I shall have employment the same as if it were summer. I am writing in my room all alone with the tick tick of my little clock I wish you were here Stella that I might tell you how happy I am but then I hope you will take it all for granted I only hope that you are sharing somewhat in it. Let me see! you said unless something happens between now and then. Well! That gives me lots of comfort because you know things don't happen at all because they are ordained Well! I dont see as I have any news to write I haven't seen any of my people since I got back I would like to go up that way next Sat. but hardly think I shall I don't like to be away from town every Sunday I don't think now it will be a great many weeks before you will see me at Sparta again. I suppose it would be impossible for me to be with you Christmas but I know no reason why I can't come down some Sat. before that. Why! Just think it was only a little over 2 hours from the time we started from the house Monday untill I was in the office at work. Have you heard from Irva yet. I dread to think that there is a possibility of your going back again to DuBois. perhaps that is selfish but it is so much farther away that's all Well! you must try and not be lonesome and write promptly and I'll try to do the same. Good Night with a kiss and God bless you Stella.
Norman W. Ingerson

V

it is all for the best

Norman and Stella exchange seventy-five letters in the year before their marriage. The sheer bulk of this correspondence, as well as its intimacy of thought and experience, vividly expose their lives during that year. Stella's proximity in Sparta makes her easily accessible to Norman. Despite his frequent visits, she is increasingly isolated by the requirements of care for her ailing father. Death claims three members of Stella's family in 1896. Through this extremely difficult year, she relies on Norman for comfort and support.

Meanwhile, Norman is assuming a well-rounded Victorian respectability in Jamestown. His wages keep pace with his responsibilities at the Jamestown Cotton Mill. He is active both in civic and in church-related affairs and secure in his Christian orthodoxy. Now at the beginning of his twenty-third year, he has achieved an independence for which he is proud. For such a young man in Victorian America, marriage is the next logical step. Norman has never doubted the institution, nor does he question his readiness for it. His letters in 1896 reveal an emotional maturity. Faced with Stella's emotional need, culminating with her father's death, he assumes a control born out of loving concern for her. Stella enters marriage in mourning, Norman with the eagerness and the confidence necessary to take responsibility for his and his bride's happiness.

Stella's twenty-third birthday at brother Will's home in Spartansburg. She is nursing Rose and the baby Frank, the youngest of Will's three children. Her Aunt is Jennie, Uncle Lon Murdock's wife. Norman is worried Irva will call Stella back to work in Dubois.

Spartansburg,
Nov 29th 1895
Dear Norman: –
I received your very welcome letter last Tuesday. I am at Will's to-night came down this afternoon Rose is sick and so I don't know how long I will have to stay. I got home at about noon the day you went away and the next day I went up to my Aunts and stayed there a couple of nights – had a very nice time. No! I haven't had a letter from Irva yet. I dont' think there is any danger of my going back there very soon. I am glad you think you can come down again before Christmas I only wish you could come oftener but of course I know you can't.–Well! to-day is my birthday and not a very enjoyable one I can assure you. I will try and finish this letter later.
Dec. 2nd
Well! Norman I will write a few more lines this morning. Rose is very low and the baby has been sick too so you can imagine what a time we are having. It keeps Will and I busy nearly all the time to do the work and wait on her and the children. It is snowing hard here to-day think we can have a sleigh ride next time you are out. Well! Norman You must excuse this miserable letter this time and write very soon
Yours lovingly
Stella
Pen & ink is scarce here.

Jamestown,
December 3, 1895
Tuesday Eve
Dear Stella –
I received your letter to day. Was sorry to hear that Rose is sick I
hope she will soon be better. I am afraid you will get sick if you
have to stay there and be up nights. I am at the office writing,
thought I had better answer your letter to night as I am booked
for every evening except Saturday for the rest of the week tomorrow evening is prayer-meeting and Thursday there is a
Commiteemans Banquet at the Y.M.C.A. Rooms at 6-30 P.M. and I
expect to be there if nothing happens. I think I told you about the
Educational classes at the Y.M.C.A. did I not. Well! the class in
bookkeeping which meets every Friday eve got too large for one
teacher and I have been appointed as Assistant so you see there
goes Friday Evening. I get 50 cents per week for it though so you
see I am helped by it nevertheless. I was down to Mart's and
stayed a week ago last Saturday night They are getting along first
rate as far as finances are concerned. He has taken the school for
the year Thanksgiving I went up to my sisters. I had a good time
George's people were there too and also father. I think if nothing
happens to prevent that I shall be down to see you Saturday Dec.
14 I am counting the days but they will soon pass I suppose. I
think I can realize something of how hard a position you are
placed in Stella but you must have courage it's a long road that
has no turn, you know. Well as I am nearly finishing this sheet
will close for this time. please answer very soon,
Good Night
with love
Norman

Death of Rose.

Spartansburg, Pa.
Dec 9th 1895
Dear Norman: –
Your letter which found us in great sorrow received a short time
ago. Rose died Wed. night at 6 oclock and was buried Friday,
funeral was at the house. poor girl no one but God knows what
she suffured. I hope I shall never have to witness so much suffering again. I expect to stay here until we can get things straight-
ened around and I will get some place for the children, poor little
things don't seem to realize what they have lost. I guess Pa will
take the baby and Uncle Lons folks may take one. Rose sister is
here helping me she did not get here in time to see her alive she
feels very bad. Well Norman I would love to have you come
down next Sat if I could be at home but I can't tell yet when I can
be so guess you will have to wait a week or two longer. Yesterday
was quarterly meeting here Will and I went Well Goodby for this
time hopeing to hear from you soon
 I remain as ever your loving friend, Stella
(Excuse the lead pencil & paper.)

Jamestown, N.Y.
Dec 11 1895
Dear Stella, –
I received your letter just before dinner. I was painfully surprized
to hear that Rose is dead. I can't help thinking of the poor little
children. What a terrible thing it is for them to be left motherless.
I am at the office it is one o'clock P.M. I could not wait till
evening before anwering, so I am stealing the time. I was down
to Martie's and stayed last Saturday night, "Aunt Addie" Cobb is
staying there and doing the housework. Last Wednesday was
Mart's Father's & Mother's 23rd year wedding anniversary. He
and I went up there in the Evening we left here about 6 o'clock
and had to be up all night in order to get back in the morning.
How little I knew what was transpiring at that time where you
was. If I had known I should have not have enjoyed the thing
very much I don't think. Well, Stella I hope you will not get

sick.You must be careful and take good care of yourself as well as to care for others, I wish you could hear our new Minister, I like him better every time I hear him. He gave a grand talk last Sunday evening. After the sermon, there were three baptized and in the aftermeeting which we held there was 3 came forward. Well! I am sorry it is not possible for me to come to see you next Sat. but will come as soon as you write me you are at home. I think I can come either the 21st or the 28th if you get home by that time. As I have lots of work to do I will close for this time Write very soon
Yours lovingly
Norman
S.W.A.K.

Disposition of Will's children. The little girl, Rilla, is taken in by neighbors. Later she will join Will in Dubois (letter, Oct. 8, 1896).

Spartansburg, Pa
Dec. 17th 95.
Dear Norman: –
I am at home again at last came back last Sat. night. It seems good to get back again. I had gotten pretty well tired out. Rose sister went on the 1-16 train Sat. morning she was very good to help me don't know what I would have done if she hadnt I guess Will will go out to work for Irva again. Uncle Lons folks have Lyric and one of our neighbors the little girl and the baby is with us he is good but requires a great deal of care I find. I guess there is no danger now of my going back to Du Bois even if they should want me. I would like to have you come out a week from Sat. the 28th I think I could entertain you better than next Sat. Frankie is quite contented here, he can talk some. I havn't been to church but 2 or 3 times since you was here was at quarterly meeting in the burg but some way I didn't enjoy the sermon much. As I know of nothing very interesting to write away out here in the country will close hoping to hear from you soon and also see you the 28th.
Yours lovingly
Stella.

Jamestown, N.Y.
Dec.19-95
Dear Stella,
Your very welcome letter received to day was glad to hear you
are home again. We are having very warm weather for December
aren't we? I don't like it very well myself. I prefer snow and
sleighing dont you? Do you know today is my birthday it doesn't
seem to make a great deal of difference with me though in fact I
nearly forgot about it myself until I was changeing the Dater in
the office this morning. I was up to George's Sunday they are all
well. I went on the 2-45 train Sat. afternoon. but when I came
back I skated to Lakewood, a distance of about four miles and
then came on the Street Car. I found I was not a very strong
skater this winter in fact I got so tired I walked the last half mile.
Well! Stella it is almost Christmas and do you know I almost
dread it because I want to get Presents for so many and feel so
very poor. I have not had another increase in my wages but hope
that the beginning of the New Year may bring one. how thankful
I ought to be though that I am not situated as I was last winter.
Where do you expect to be Christmas day? Kate wanted me to go
to her mother's Mrs. Reardon's at Mayville but I don't know yet
but I may have to work on that day taking Inventory. And: by the
way I am quite sure that I can come down on the 28th as it is the
end of the year and our Semi Anual statement has to be gotten
off But! you may be sure I shall come if I can possibly get away
"Good Night,"
Friday Morn,
Well Stella I am at the office and will add a few words in closing I
think probably I can come a week from tomorrow. You must
write as soon as you receive this and I will write you again before
then. I have just found out that I will not have to work Xmas. I
wish I could be with you but that is impossible I suppose. Well I
must draw this poor excuse of a letter to a close.
write soon
A Merry Christmas
with love
Norman

The Murdocks live in the country outside of Spartansburg. Going to the "burg" means going to the village. Union is a village northwest of Spartansburg. Norman and Stella must have taken a sleigh ride to Union during Norman's visit in January 1895. Britton Run, a crossroads about a mile from the farm, is home to three churches and a store. Eugene is a Sparta acquaintance.

A Merry Xmas,
Spartansburg, Pa.
Dec. 25th-95
Dear Norman,
I received your welcome letter last Sunday. Dot went to the burg Sat. and it rained so that she stayed all night. Well! to day is Christmas and I am spending it at home I wish you could be here it doesn't seem much like Christmas to me. I suppose you are at Mrs. Reardons hope you will have a good time. Isn't this gloomy weather it is raining here to day. We just heard that Joe Emersons were all burnt out that is where we stopped for dinner the day we went to Union. They saved some of their goods. I hope you can come out Saturday I would have answered your letter before but the roads are so bad did not get any chance to mail it. There was a Christmas tree at Britton Run last evening but I did not go am sorry now that I didn't I guess it was quite good for Britton Run. Well Eugene is waiting for this letter so I will close hoping to see you next Saturday.
I am as ever your friend
Stella.
In haste

Tuesday, written following Norman's weekend visit. The visit is his first since his proposal. The Chautauqua Lake Railway has ceased Sunday operations for the winter.

A Happy New Year
Jamestown
Dec 31 1895
Dear Stella,
I arrived safely yesterday at a little after ten and found everything all right it doesn't seem to make a great deal of difference if
I am here or not but I think perhaps if I was to stay away 2 weeks
instead of 2 days there would be more difference Has your head
stopped aching yet? I found that I did not feel very gay yesterday. but I went to bed about 9 last night and got a good nights
rest and feel quite like myself now. Where do you expect to be
tomorrow? I expect to work tomorrow most of the day at least.
There is going to be a reception at the Y.M.C.A. Rooms in the
afternoon and evening dont know yet whether I will go or not as
it is prayer meeting night and I do not like to miss that. I have
not seen any of my folks since I came back and dont know when
it will be so I can go up that way as I see by the papers that there
will be no Sunday trains on that road this winter. Stella do you
remember where we were 3 years ago to night and how the bells
rang at Midnight. Well! There have many things happened since;
that I am sorry about, but many more that I am thankful for and
most of all I thank God that I, (as I believe) am living nearer to
him, and the mistakes I have made have led me to ask mercy of
him rather than to be discouraged by them and fail utterly. There
is going to be a party at the Methodist church this Evening to
watch the old year out but I dont think I shall be seen there. I
wish you was here we'd go up wouldn't we When I sat down to
write I didn't think I could find much to say but I see I have
filled the sheet for all that. so I will close hoping to hear from you
very soon.
I am yours with love
Norman

The new year finds Stella in fine spirits. She and Norman spent New Year's Eve, 1892, together in Dubois. Norman certainly understands that one of the things Stella has not yet "regreted" is his proposal.

Spartansburg, Pa.
Jan 7th 1896
Dear Norman,
Hello there old boy. How are you? How do you like such cold weather we have quite good sleighing here now or at least I guess it is. I went to one of our neighbors yesterday on a load of wood and thought it was fine. I think we can have a sleigh ride when you come again. My! but haven't we had some blustery days since you was here? I went to the burg friday and you may believe I was not very sorry when I reached home again it reminded me of the day we went to Union only a great deal worse. Yes! I remember plainly where we were three years ago New Years eve, and, as you say there have been a great many things happened since that I am sorry for and some that I have not as yet regreted. I am quite sorry that Phill and I had the trouble we did but don't think I shall let it worry me much. Ethie is married and gone to Ohio with her husband was married the day before Christmas so I heard, was married in York State. so you see there is another chance for you gone. It has been only a week yesterday since you was here but it seems more like two to me. Time I believe seemed shorter when I was in Du Bois. Well! I will quit before I weary you too much.
Good by
Yours with love
Stella.

To "improve" the sleighing, in Norman's sense, is to take advantage of it. "Grass widow" is a rather pejorative term for a married woman, now unattached, whose husband is still alive. Norman's mother is a grass widow.

Jamestown,
Jan 9-96
Dear Stella,
How do you do this evening. "I am quite well thank you and hope these few lines will find you the Same" Well Stella! I received your letter this noon. I don't know as I ought to answer it so soon but think I will just the same as tomorrow Eve, is my night at theY.M.C.A. bookkeeping class Yes! we have good sleighing here too. I just wish I might improve it more I hope you may be able to do so. I have been very busy since I got back, I worked during the fore noon of New Years day. Then in the afternoon I attended a reception at the Y.M.C.A. Rooms. It is 9 o'clock and as I am very tired. Let's say good night
Friday morning
Well! Stella
I will try and write you a little more I am quite surprized to hear that Ethie was married I hope she has made a good choice. I am glad to tell you I am now getting nine dollars per week instead of eight and Mr. Smith sort of half promised that it would be increased again before very long. I think if nothing happens I will go up to George's tomorrow. wish you might be there too we could have a sleigh ride I think. Mart was in here last Sat. His school began again on Mon. last He says it is a settled thing that Mattie is to be married next June. Oh! dear! there goes another chance. but then I don't suppose I ought to be discouraged. Mr. Hall the machinist says there is a grass widow come to work here this morning and he don't suppose that my girl will stand much of a chance after this. Perhaps I have scribbled about enough of nonsense. and as I am writing on T.H. Smith's time will close
Write very soon
Yours, lovingly
Norman

Spartansburg, Pa.
Jan 18-96
Dear Norman, –
With pleasure I will now answer your very welcome letter of a
short time ago. My folks have gone over to Joe Emersons and
Frank and I are keeping house. I was to town yesterday went up
to the house and swept it out and how lonesome it did seem
without Rose. I guess Pa will rent the place down there this summer. I almost wish he was going to move down himself instead.
Well! I thought this morning that we were going to lose our
sleighing but it is snowing now. We expect Irva out about the 1st
of next month. I got a letter from Eliza and what do you think!
Phil sent his best regards to me. I suppose you and the grass
widow you spoke of are firm friends by now are you not? Edna
and Evart were up last Sunday we had a splendid visit. Norman
I wish I could go to church with you to morrow, if you were here
we might go down to Britton Run again. wouldn't that be fine?
Well I will close for this time. hoping to hear from you very soon.
I don't know as you can read this my pen is so poor, if you can't
just return C.O.D. Good by
Your loving friend.
Stella

Norman's sleigh ride with his father begins at George's farm near Bemus Point.
They probably crossed the lake on the ice to Celeron where Norman picked up a
Chautauqua Traction car to Jamestown.

Jamestown,
Jan 21,–96
Dear Stella,
I received your very welcome letter this morning. I dont know as
I ought to answer it so soon, but guess I will not wait as long as
you did. I am not very busy lately since I got through with our
Semi Annual Closing. In fact the work becomes easier for me
every day as I get more used to it. I went up to Georges and
stayed last Saturday night. Had a very nice visit and returned in
time to attend church in The Evening Stella I wish you might

have been there. I think it was one of the best sermons I ever heard. I received a check of $2 for my services in the Bookkeeping class during Dec. It will be quite a help to me and I hardly know that I have spent any time on it either Do you expect that Irva will stay a great while. I wish it might be so I could see him. Aren't we having nice winter weather though? The sleighing is very good up here. I had quite a nice sleigh ride Sunday There are no Sunday trains on that road so Father brought me to Celeron and I came from there on a street-car. There is to be an Entertainment in the Opera House next Thurs. evening for the benefit of the Y.M.C.A. Educational Classes I wish you could be here and go. I tell you Stella it makes me feel mean when I think how you are obliged to stay out in the country and how I have so many priveliges, which you do not. but as I have said before it's a long road that has no turning. Well! some how I can think of nothing very interesting to write so I will close for this time hoping to hear from you very, very, soon
I remain as ever
Norman

Cousin Dollie Gray, daughter of Alonzo and Lucinda Gray, is Stella's most cherished childhood friend. Alonzo Gray is Stella's deceased mother's brother. He is identified in Stella's letters as "Uncle Lon Gray." Pa's brother is also named Alonzo. "Uncle Lon" refers to Alonzo Murdock. The Grays moved from Sparta to Titusville shortly before the courtship began.

Spartansburg, Pa.
Jan 29-96
Dear Norman:–
Received your most welcome letter a few days ago which I read with pleasure and will try and write you a few lines this eve but don't know what in the world to write. Well! I wish you was here we might have went to an oyster supper to night about two miles from here. I wanted to go but my best fellow didn't come after me. What lovely evenings we are having now aren't we? Yes! I wish too that you might see Irva when he comes out but I don't know when he will come and don't know how long he will stay but I suppose not very long. I look for him some next Sat. My

cousin Dollie Gray and Aunt Deal Davis were here to visit me a
week ago to-day I had not seen her (Dollie) since before I went to
the grape country (if I remember rightly) She lives about five
miles from Titusville. Dot has been to an Aid Society to day, Pa
went to a sale and Frank and I stayed at home like good children.
Pa is sick most of the time lately he is doctoring with a different
Doctor now and I am in hopes will soon be better. When do you
think you can come out? Well! I guess I will close for this time
hoping to hear from you very soon
"Good night"
from you loving friend
Estella.

Jamestown, N.Y.
Jan 31, 1896.
Dear Stella,
Your very welcome letter at hand and guess I will give it an
immediate answer as usual. I have been very busy all day getting
the Pay Roll ready but having a few spare minutes I will gladly
give them to you. Yes we are having fine evenings and I wish you
lived in Jamestown I would try and influence that Best Fellow of
yours to come around oftener if I could find him. Well! Stella I
am some like you I hardly know what to write. I should have
waited till this evening to write this but see it is the night the
Book-keeping Class meets. One week ago last night I attended an
Entertainment in the opera house it was one of the numbers on
the Y.M.C.A. Lecture Course Last Tuesday Eve I was at the M.E.
Church to a Concert which I think was the greatest musical treat I
ever heard. I will enclose a program and that will explain better
than I can How I wish you might have heard it. Well! Wednesday
night I attended prayer meeting of course and last night I was
obliged to attend the annual meeting and Election of officers at
our Young Peoples Society After the Business part was transacted
We all retired to the Sunday School Room where some of the
ladies had prepared a banquet after the supper a number of
Toasts were responded to by members of the Society. My! but
"aint" I giving a pretty strict account of myself though. Well

Stella! I think I may come down to see you about one week from to-morrow Feb. 8. providing you do not think it is too soon to be proper. I hope you will excuse me for scribbling so. and write very soon
Your loving Freind
Norman

Written at the cotton mill following Norman's weekend visit. The "proper" spacing of visits for an engaged couple is an issue of Victorian etiquette.

Jamestown
Feb 10 1896
Dear Stella.
How are you feeling this afternoon. If you are any like me you are just a trifle sleepy. I dont believe I have very much to write but am going to nevertheless so as to get a reply sooner Well! we didn't have a bit of trouble getting to the train this morning. I arrived at the office at 10 o'clock and every-thing was running along quite smoothly. The sun is shining and it is a very pleasant afternoon here. How I wish we might take a sleighride. I think there is more snow up here than at the 'Burg. Well Stella! I really haven't anything to write and as It is Smith's time I will close hoping to hear from you very soon.
I remain
Yours with love
Norman

Spartansburg, Pa.
Feb 15th 96
Saturday Evening
Dear Norman.
I just rec'd your very welcome letter yesterday. How are you feel-ing by this time? I am just about sick with a cold. Pa went to Du Bois this morning or rather started this morning, he stayed at Uncle Lons last night and went from there. Irva did not know of his coming. I guess he will be gone about a week. My! but it

seems lonesome here without him. I wish you was here. Norman I don't believe you enjoyed your last visit very much did you just one week ago to-day wasn't it, does that mean 5 or 7 more weeks. I hope not more than that - but - you know best. The roads have been drifted terribly since Monday I suppose you have had about the same kind of weather there as we have had very stormy. Well Norman I don't know of anything worth writing so will close hoping to hear from you very soon and a good long letter.

"Good night"

Ever Yours

Stella

Jamestown, N.Y.

Feb. 19, 1896

My Dear Stella –

I am in receipt of your most welcome letter and am going to give you an immediate answer. I am sorry to hear you are not feeling quite well and hope that this may find you feeling "O.K." I am surprized to hear your father has gone to Du Bois. I hope he will feel better while there than he did 3 years ago. I was up to my sisters and stayed last Saturday night I had a real good visit, and wish you might have been there too. In fact Stella I'm always wishing that whereever I go. Martie was up last Sat. forenoon and called on me at the office. I haven't been down there since before Christmas and suppose I ought to go before long. I lent him $20 which he was obliged to borrow on account of not being able to get any more of his Salary until some time in April. It is about 2 o'clock P.M. and I am writing as you see on my employers time but know it will be all right because I am not very busy lately. in fact there are some days I can hardly find enough to do to keep busy. The Mill is running till 7 p.m. every day this week excepting next Sat. when it will be closed to do some repairing. I do not expect to work then how I wish I could be, with you Stella. of course that is impossible; So, you think I did not enjoy my visit very well do you? Well I will have to inform you that you are mistaken. I only wish I might have stayed longer.

If nothing happens I do not think it will be more than 5 weeks
from last Saturday till I shall come again. I certainly hope it will
be no longer. Well! Stella I see I am nearing the end of this sheet
so I suppose I must say Goodbye for this time
I remain Yours with love
Norman
write soon

*Brother Will appears to have been a black sheep in Stella's estimation. Will is
five years older than Stella. Pa's start in Christian life may have had something
to do with feelings of mortality surrounding his chronic ill health.*

Spartansburg, Pa
Mar 6th '96
Dear Friend: –
I will now embrace a few moments in answer to your very welcome letter of some time ago and hope to receive a more prompt
reply than I am giving you. Pa came home the next Saturday
from Du Bois had a pleasant time while there but has been very
sick since he came back. The Doctor was here yesterday to see
him Will came home a week ago last Saturday and went away
again Monday he has quit working for the man he was working
for and is canvassing for himself now. He had a good chance if
he had only stuck to it. It is raining hard here to-day I did intend
going to town but guess I will have to give it up. Pa met a man in
Du Bois that is accquainted with you a Mr. Lute. I believe he said
his name was. Revival meetings are being held in Britton Run. I
have been but two nights. The preacher Mr. Black and a few others were here the other day for dinner we had prayer, singing
and a real good visit and Norman I am so glad to tell you that Pa
has made a start in a Christian life. Well! It will soon be spring
and I am so glad this has seemed like such a long winter but I am
not the least bit sorry that I spent it at home instead of Du Bois I
was at first but don't believe I am now. Well Norman I must
bring this poor excuse of a letter to a close hoping to hear from
you very soon. I remain Yours with love
Stella

Jamestown N.Y.

Mar. 9 1896

Dear Stella,

Your most welcome and long looked for letter received last Saturday. I was very glad to know you are well; for Stella I had about made up my mind you was sick because you did not write sooner. But then I can readily see that it is much easier for me having writing material before me all of the time to snatch a few minutes in which to write a letter than it is for you. I am sorry to hear your father is sick and hope he may soon get better. it is his same old complaint I suppose. My Brother was down and took dinner with me today. I was up there two weeks ago last Saturday and had a very good visit came back in the evening in time for church We have such good services every sunday I wish you could be here and go too. There are Revival services being held in the Methodist Church this week. I think I may go this evening Tomorrow night is the last number on the Y.M.C.A. Lecture Course. I wish you might be here and go with me. it is a concert by the Boston Ariel Quartet Well Stella I can't find much of Interest to write so please excuse this poorly scribbled letter and write soon

Yours with love

Norman

S.W.A.K.

Birth of Nora Dorne's first child. Nora married early in 1894 (letter, Feb. 2, 1894).

Spartansburg,

Mar 12-96

Dear Norman

Received your very welcome letter yesterday and guess I will give you a surprise by writing immediately, hope the shock will not overcome you so that you will not be able to work. Well if it is as stormy in Jamestown as it is here this morning you will need to have a good grip on your hat. Pa has not been feeling as well for the last few days but I think is some better this morning.

I think we will change Doctors if he does not get better before long. Meeting closed at Britton Run last evening in the Methodist church and commenced in the Brethren. They met with quite good success well there is nothing much to write about as usual O yes! Nora Dorn has a little daughter
Good bye
Your loving friend,
Stella
s.w.a.k.

Jamestown, N.Y.
Mar. 16, 1896
3 P.M.
Dear Stella,
Your most welcome letter received to day. You did surprize me a little by answering so soon and I think I had better return the compliment I am sorry your father doesnt get along faster and hope when you write again you will have better news in regard to him It is fine sleighing here but it doesnt seem to make much difference in my Business. My! but I would like to take a sleigh ride. Well! Stella I don't know of much to write. I don't think I will come down next Sat. but will wait a couple of weeks until old Winter quits lingering in the lap of Spring. The Evangelist of whom I wrote as being at the M.E. Church was taken sick 2 or 3 days after he came and has not been able to conduct the meeting but the Pastor has taken it up and I guess they have been quite successful thus far. Well! Stella as I have survived this surprize so well you need not be afraid of trying it again but write very soon to
Your loving
Norman

Death of Frank Murdock, two-years-old. Stella's graphic description of the child's last days is typically Victorian. The death, heavy winter, and her father's illness magnify Stella's isolation.

Spartansburg, Pa.
Mar 23-'96
7 p.m.
My Dear Norman,
It is with great sorrow I sit down to answer yours of to day. We have looked upon that dear little face of Frankie's for the last time on this earth. He came down with the measles a week ago yesterday and was up around until Friday night when he was taken with bleeding from the nose and vomiting blood, also passed blood caused the Doctor said from a hemorage of the bowels. the measles having taken that course, and died Saturday morning at, a quarter past two after intense suffering. It seems so hard for us to give up the dear little soul but it was Gods will and while we know he can never return to us we have this to console us that we can go to him. The funeral was held at the house to day at 11 oclock Text 2nd Samuel 12-23. Norman it seems to me now that he was one of the sweetest children that ever lived. I am so lonely without that dear little fellow and to think we haven't even a picture of him. I thought of telegraphing to you but thought I had heard you say you had not had the measles. Pa I think in some respects is a little better but of course this trouble makes him worse he is not able to go out doors any yet. Norman I would like so much to see you but think too you had better wait until the weather is better and I hope that will not be long. The road we live on is dreadfully drifted in places and on the other roads there is scarcely any sleighing at all Well! my dear, good night for this time and write very soon to your loving Stella.

Franklin "Pa" Murdoch

Pa Murdock to Mr. Weaver, Rose's father.

Sparta
March 25/1896
Mr. Weaver
it is with a verrey sad hart that I take pen in hand to let you
know of the deth of hower Dear little boy Frankey he was as well
as could be til about one weak before he dide he had the mesels
the docter said he never saw them coime out better about the
forth day his nose took to bleding they had quite a time to stop it
and after they did hemreg of the bowels set in and he didn't last
but a verry short time but as long as we could endure to sea the
dear little thing suffer O you cannot amagen how wee miss him
how sweatly he would kiss us good night and then go upstares
and sing him selfe to sleap but wee hav one thing to comfort and
that is he is with the god that gave him and wee never can call
him back but wee can go to him Blessed be the Lord, now the
most strang thing about this is how he came to hav the measels
but wee think will must brot them in he came home about the
rite time altho the other children did not take it but he tok
Frankey in bed with him Mr. Weaver it is with a grate effert that I
write to you at all for I am verry porley I hav not bin out for
three weaks but I feal as if I must tel you my selfe I know you
will all feal verry sad how strang it seams to me to think that

Rose and Frankey ar ded and no picture of them tel Jessey wee recieved her letter Monday the day of the funerel dide Saturday morning at a quarter past two oclock wee sent you a dispach the same morning which I presume you recieved giv my love to all your familey and wright soon
this from your ever trew friend
F.W. Murdock

Jamestown N.Y.
Mar 25, 1896
3-30 p.m.
Dear Stella,
I received your letter today and I hardly know how to write a reply that will express my feelings Yes! It is sad news to me Stella. How hard it is for us in such a time to say, "Thy will be done." I think perhaps it is as well that you did not telegraph to me but if you had I should certainly have come. Stella you don't know how I long to be with you but as next Sat. is Payday I think it is wisest to wait until a week from then April 4th when I shall surely be down. Did Irva's folks come out to the funeral? I suppose of course that Will was there what is he doing now? I was down to Martin's and stayed last Sat. night the first time I have been there this year, he says Fred Smith (Mattie's fellow you know) has bought out the blacksmith shop where he was working, and he talked to Mart as though there might be a wedding up on the hill before long. Well! Stella I hope in reply to this you may be able to send a letter full of Good news. I hope you won't get sick but I cant help worrying about you just a little. I am glad to tell you that I am to receive $10 per week hereafter. It seems to me as I look back and see where I was a year ago that I cannot thank God enough for the way he has blessed me it is certainly more than I deserve and believe me Stella I count you not as the least of these blessings.
Good bye for this time my darling and may God Bless You
Norman
Write soon
Isaiah 41-10

John Richardson, a hired man, will be mentioned in future letters.

Spartansburg, Pa.
Mar 31st '96
Dear Norman,
Your kind and welcome letter received a few days ago am very glad you are coming out Saturday but can't promise you a very pleasant time. Pa is no better is in a great deal of pain this morning. I am very much worried about him. I tell you he looks pretty poorly. I think we will have a counsel of Doctors this week, if he is not better in a day or so. Will is at home now and John Richardson commenced working Mon. I guess Eugene will go home to-morrow he is helping us wash to day. No! Irva's folks were not to Frankie's funeral he has been real sick but was better the last I heard from him. Well! I will close. hoping to see you soon,
Good bye,
Stella

Jamestown
Apr. 1, 1896
Dear Stella.
I do not know that you will get this before Saturday but thought I would write and let you know for sure that I will be down on the afternoon train next Saturday if nothing happens. I went to a meeting in the Methodist Church last night. The same Evangilist that was there two or three weeks ago is still there he spoke last night upon the Modern dance. It is the first sermon I ever heard on the subject and I was very much pleased with it Well Stella! I will not try to write much today but will say more when I see you good bye for this time.
Your loving
Norman

Monday afternoon. Norman's third weekend visit since his proposal. His mention of a brief visit to Evart Frost indicates that Stella did not accompany him to the depot in Spartansburg. Apparently, Norman's boarding house has a telephone to which Frances intends to call for news of Stella's father. Frances' "doing her work alone" implies that she lacks a hired girl. Norman's bicycle remains at the Cheney house where he left it after being caught in a snowstorm (letter, Oct. 21, 1895).

Jamestown, N.Y.
Apr 6-1896
Dear Stella.
I arrived safely at 10 o'clock this morning, and found my work in very good shape. Have been quite busy but will take a few minutes in which to write to you. Mr. Smith is at the office to day. I stopped in at Evart Frost's 2 or 3 minutes this morning and had a nice little chat I think they are both just nice, and how happy they seem to be together. Frances said last Friday that she would telephone home to day and find out how your father was but I guess she has forgotten about it. "She is doing her work alone and I suppose can't leave the children alone to go to the neighbors who has the phone." I did not mean this for poetry. I think I shall go up there next Sat. and bring my bicycle down here; and ride on the pavement some in the evenings for exercise. Well Stella! I really can't think of much to write I hope your father is feeling better to night. I can just imagine now that it is suppertime and I can see you Stella anticipating his every want and waiting on him like the good angel that you are. I would almost be willing to be sick if I could have you take care of me. Well! It is now half past five and I will say goodbye for this time and get ready to go to my supper
write very soon to
your loving, Norman

Frequent visitations at the Murdock household underscore the seriousness of Pa's condition. "Your Aunt" probably refers to Aunt Lucinda Gray's affection for Norman.

Spartansburg, Pa
April, 13th 1896.
Dear Norman,
Do not think I have forgotten you entirely. I have been very busy or would have written sooner. Pa has been a great deal worse since you was here. The pain he suffered last night was something terrible. He is very weak has sit up but very little to day Norman you don't know how I long to see him well, again. Edna & Evart were up yesterday. Irva went away Friday I took him to the train and we stayed at Evart's for dinner. Isn't this lovely weather? The roads are drying up quite fast. Did you go up to your sisters Saturday? (Your Aunt) Lucinda came the day you went away and stayed until Wed. She said she would like to have seen you. Dot and I both feel today as though we would like a hired girl if we could get a good one. Well! Norman this letter will have to be rather short as Will is about ready to go to the burg
Write very soon to your loving
Stella.

Jamestown
Apr 17 – 1896
Dear Stella,
I just received your very welcome letter to day, as It was written Monday I dont understand why it didn't get here sooner. I am dissapointed to hear your father is worse for somehow I had thought he would be better before this and I hope this will find him improving. My! but aren't we having warm weather for April The mercury stands at 78 in the office. Yes! I went up to my sisters Sat. and in the evening went up to George's Kate was sick but is getting better I brought my wheel down with me Sunday eve and have been riding some this week. Last night I went up to my sister's and stayed it is about 8 miles up there. I started from

— 120 —

there at half past five this morning and got here a little before half past 6 The roads are quite dry but not very smooth yet. Mart has taken the school at Dewittville to teach for a couple of weeks during his vacation while the regular teacher is away. It is there that Mattie is be be married May 13, her "affianced" was here yesterday on his way up there. He wanted to know if I had received an Invitation so I suppose I will get one. He also spoke of your coming up. I wish it might be possible for you to come Stella. Kate said tell you to come and stay a week or two Mr. Smith is now president of the Young Mens Christian Association. We held our annual meeting and election last Mon. Evening, Well Stella I have written about all the news I can think of. Tell your father to keep up good grit and get well as fast as he can. I will be down in a few weeks and would like to see him at the train to meet me. I must say goodby for this time write very soon to your loving,
Norman.
P.S. Forgive me Stella but if your Father should be a great deal worse and you wanted to send me word quickly, direct in care of the Jamestown Cotton Mill.
Yours lovingly & prayerfully
Norman

Spartansburg, Pa
April 20-'96
Dear Norman,
Received your letter Saturday. I think Pa is a very little better to-day. We have changed Doctors and I think the one we have now is going to help him. We had counsel of Doctors again last Thursday and Dr. Kibler of Corry claimed that there was some-thing in his side and would have to have an operation before he could get well but we could not consent to such a thing not knowing whether it would kill or cure him unless we knew it to be the last resort so we got a Doctor from a different school and he says it is not necessary. if that is only so, he can help him. God only knows how happy we will be He sits up some in bed but is not able to be dressed. Norman I suppose you would not have

had my letter yet if I had not happened to have seen it among some old ones Will was looking over he went to the burg three times and never mailed it and finally I sent it by John I intend going to the burg this afternoon so I guess you will get this. I would like very much (if I should be invited) to attend Mattie's wedding but of course that will be impossible unless Pa should be a great deal better. My Uncle Albert Gray is here to-day I guess there were about a dozen here yesterday to see Pa. Joe Emerson was here. he is going to start for Colorado to-morrow if I was his wife I don't believe I would let him go. Well Norman I hope you will have a good time at the wedding congratulate Mattie for me. Well I must close or I will not get to the burg very soon You must excuse this horribly scribbled letter for I write it in a great hurry Good by,
Write soon
Your loving,
Stella

Victorian fatalism clearly expressed.

Jamestown, N.Y.
Apr. 22-96
Dear Stella,
I received your kind and welcome letter to day, it is 15 min of 5 o'clock P.M. Mr Smith has gone up town and I am left alone so I will just take advantage of a few quiet minutes to reply. I am very sorry to hear your father gets along so slowly and hope the new Physician you speak of may be given wisdom from that greater One above to know just what to do. Stella you don't know how I wish you lived near enough so that I could drop in and see you oftener. but I expect it is best as it is or it would not be so. I think now of coming down May 30 as the Mill will probably not run that day and it being Sat. also. Fred Smith stopped here the other day and left the invitation. I think I will just send it to you and you can see "how as you" are invited I think it is a strange way to do but you know Mattie is queer about some things. What do you think will be nice to get her for a present? I do hope your

father will be so much better by that time that you can come,
Mart is at his school again began last Monday. Well! Stella I have
scribbled about all I have time to
Good bye and
write soon to your loving
Norman

From Irva Murdock.

DuBois, Pa.
May 2 1896
Dear Sister
Received your leter last night sory to hear that Pa is not geting
along faster tell him he must not get discouraged for the com-
plant has ben coming a good while and it will probly take a long
time to get controle of it. how I wish I was closer by so I could se
him more often I want you to drop me a card every weak for I
keep woring about him all the time when I dont hear I am not a
bit well my self I have Rheumatism quite bad and cant get no
sleap nights. I am a shamed to think I cant send father the money
for the buter I will send it this month about the last. We have a
large amount of work going out this month and we are terrbly
rushed. Jack has ben sick but is working now he is back the Dr
advised him to leave Buffalo how I wish you could se our new
place it is fine I tell you tell Will that we will get his work out as
quick as possible our moving has put us a little behind on all
work
Yours Truly
I.F. Murdock

Spartansburg, Pa.
May 2 – '96
Dear Norman:
If you was here this afternoon I am quite sure I could think of
enough to talk about but I dont know what in the world I am
going to write. Pa is not much if any better I am just about discouraged about him (some times). He has been in a great deal of
pain to day. You would be surprised to see how very poor he is.
about all the nourishment he can take is a little milk or broth. It is
raining here this afternoon I think I will go to the burg this
evening with our hired man if it stops. Aunt Lucinda has been
with us for the past week and longer Dot took her home to-day
We went to the Commencement exercises at the burg Thursday
evening they were very nice. I wish you could have went with
me. There were five girls & five boys graduated. I would like
very much to attend the wedding but it is entirely out of the
question I really don't know what to tell you to get for a present
so guess you will have to decide for yourself. A silver sugar
spoon would be nice I guess. It is supper time and so I will close
for this time. Do not wait as long as I have before writing
Good by
Yours lovingly
Stella.

Jamestown, N.Y.
May 5, 1896
Dear Stella,
Your very welcome letter received to day, It is needless for me to
say I am sorry to hear your father is getting along so slowly. Kate
is in town today I was just up town and had quite a visit with
her. She was dissapointed to hear that you could not come to the
wedding but she said to tell you to come visiting anyhow as soon
as you could. I am thinking some of going up there to night on
my wheel, and come back early in the morning but it will depend
some on how I feel after supper. My! but aren't we having lovely
weather, I dont think I ever saw a nicer Spring. Last Sat.
Afternoon Mart. and I went up to his Father's and stayed all

night and came back Sunday just at night. We rode up on bicycles he having a borrowed one. We got caught in the rain and were just soaked when we got there. Stella I wish I could see you. If it was not Payday next Saturday I believe I should come down and you needn't be surprized to see me most any Saturday. I don't know as it will be possible for me to go to the wedding because Mr. Henry Smith is going away to England next week and there will be no one left to take my place. I spoke to Mr. Smith about it the other day and he didn't seem to think I could get away very well. Now Stella you mustn't think because you haven't much news to write that you need to wait a long time before writing. I looked for a letter from you all last week. well I have written about all I can think of that is worth writing. so good by for this time.

write soon Yours lovingly
Norman

Spartansburg,
May 11, 1896.
Dear Norman,
I will not be quite so mean this time and write sooner. Isn't this lovely weather I suppose you are making good use of your bicycle these days. Pa is feeling better to day than he did yesterday Saturday he was very bad all day. Dr. Seaburry of Sugar Grove came Friday afternoon and went away again Saturday morning we telegraphed for him he is a distant relative of ours he thinks that Pa can get up again. We look for him here again Wednesday he seems to think the Doctor we have attending him all right. I do hope they can help him soon but I am sometimes afraid that no one can but I feel a great deal more encouraged about him than I did a few days ago. Well I suppose you know by this time whether you are going to attend the wedding or not. I hope you can go. Edna & Evart have quit house-keeping and board he has moved his shop farther up town they have one room in back of it. They are going to board on account of Ednas health Dot is not very well we have a good deal to do have been washing to day and I am very tired. I will be glad to see you any Saturday you

can come. Do you think you will be out next Sat. or the 30th?
Good bye for this time & write very soon to your loving,
Stella
Pa is not feeling as well as when I commenced this letter.

Mattie Waterman and Fred Smith's wedding day. The Chadakoin River, also called the Chautauqua Outlet, flows closely behind the cotton mill. Theodore Glantz, Jr.'s body was recovered from the Outlet May 10, 1896 (Jamestown Journal, May 11, 1896).

Jamestown, N Y.
May 13,-96
Dear Stella,
Yours of the 11th received to day I am glad to receive such a prompt reply Yes! we are having nice weather this Spring It seems to me I never saw quite as nice weather at this time of year,
I was out on my wheel last evening with a friend of mine. We rode to Lake Wood and back about 4 or 5 miles I think it is. We have a Bicycle Club in the Y.M.C.A. there are 12 or 15 of us belonging tomorrow morning we are to take a run out about 6 miles to a farm house for breakfast we start at 6 o'clock and will get back about 8 I think No! I couldn't go to the wedding today. in fact I gave it up more than a week ago. I don't know Stella whether I will come down next Sat or wait until the 30th but rather think I had better wait until then as The Factory will not run that day and I can start in the morning and have longer to stay. Last Thursday one of the boys who worked here was drowned in the creek; and his body was not found until Sunday. The funeral was yesterday afternoon. The Mill shut down so that the help could go. Well! I must draw this to a close as I have got to weigh in a car of cotton. Tell your father he must try and get well fast so that I can have a big visit with him when I come down.
Good by for this time write soon to your loving
Norman

Spartansburg, Pa.
May 21, '96
Dear Norman:
Received your welcome letter a few days ago. I am glad that it is
so short a time until you can come out. I am getting anxious to
see you it has seemed like a long while since you were here. Well!
Father is just about the same if any thing a little better we think I
was frightened about him Tuesday night he awoke about 10
o'clock in the most severe pain I have seen him in since he was
sick. He said he was dying and really I didn't know but he was
How are George's people & your sisters? How nice it is that you
have a wheel and can go so much more than you could otherwise. Will went on the road again Monday & John is doing the
work alone My Aunt Lucinda is here to day we have had so
much company since Pa was sick. I have a woman here helping
us this week. How warm it is this afternoon I should think it
would be terrible in the Cotton Mill. Dr. Seaburry was here again
Tuesday, he will come again next week and stay all night I guess.
I think he is a splendid Doctor he wanted me to write and tell
him how Pa is every day he said to write just as I would to my
old spark; I wonder what he would think if he should read some
of my letters Well! I will close for this time hoping to see you here
a week from Sat.
Good bye,
Write soon
I remain "Yours" "as of old."
Stella

Jamestown, N.Y.
May 25, 1896
Dear Stella,
Your most welcome letter received Saturday I was glad to hear
your Father was even a little better and I hope this will find him
much better. I think you must be nearly tired out taking care of
him so long. I went up to George's and stayed Saturday night
Kate was visiting her mother who lives at Mayville you know. I
started from Georges about 9 o'clock yesterday morning and

rode up there got there about 10 o'clock Then I started at half past three and rode to Jamestown. I came down on the west shore of the Lake. Thus making a complete circuit of the Lake. The distance from Mayville to Jamestown is 22 miles and I came in just 2 hours and 10 minutes I have been thinking some of riding out next Saturday but have not yet decided I rather think though that I will come on the train because you know it is impossible to wear anything neat and ride a wheel. I tell you Stella I am just counting the days till Saturday and it don't seem as though I could wait. I shall come on the morning train if I can but you needn't bother about meeting me as I can walk up as well as not and I am not quite sure how I will come either. Good bye until the 30th.

Yours as ever

Norman

Spartansburg, Pa.

May 27 -'96

Dear Norman: –

Father is much worse. was taken Sat. morning with hemorage of the bowels. The Doctors think he has cancer and have but very little hopes of him if it is cancer which they think it is they say he can not get well. They have the hemorage stopped but is liable to have another any time. Norman you don't know how hard it is for me to think of giving him up. It is the worst trouble I ever tried to endure. Irva is here now. I think you better come on the train instead of your wheel.

Yours lovingly,

Stella.

Norman's note following his just completed visit is missing. Hope for Pa's recovery continues. Norman probably helped with the care during his visit so that Stella could rest. Mention of Dot's role in the care is conspicuously absent.

Spartansburg,
June 4-'96
Dear Norman: –
I received your short but sweet letter to day. I am sitting on the floor up-stairs writing and so if you can't read what I have to say don't wonder at it. There are a couple of lady's here now from the burg to see Pa. He is about the same as when you was here. I guess if anything a little better. Dr. Seabury stayed here again last night. Hasn't it been warm to-day? Well! I have slept every night and some through the day since you was here Dr. said he was glad I had got rested of course he would have something to say you know. Well if I send this to night I will have to close so I guess this will be still shorter than yours
Good by
Yours lovingly
Stella

Jamestown N.Y.
June 8, 1896
Dear Stella,
I received your welcome letter Saturday I am glad you could have a chance to sleep and get rested for I think without any jesting that you did need it. Well! Stella I am glad to hear your father is no worse and I do hope when I hear from you next it will be to say he is much better. My! but it is warm to day Mercury stands at 78 in the office this morning. but then it is quite endurable as long as it keeps below 80. It is not much as it was when I was down is it? I went up to Mark's and stayed Saturday night I had a very good time George's folks were down there Yesterday They (Cheneys) have lots of strawberries I wish you might have had some of them. It seems to me it is very early for them. Well! Stella. I was in and spent a happy hour and a half with a dentist Sat! afternoon. I had five teeth filled, but I didn't get any false ones. "honest I didn't." The Baptist Young Peoples Societies of Chaut. County met here last Tuesday and

Wednesday, and Thursday and Friday one of the Christain
Endeavorer's of the County I did not attend any in the day time but
I went to each evening meeting. There were some very good
addresses each night and one Thurs! Eve! especially I wish you
could have heard was by the Reverend Barbour of Rochester subject
Christian citizenship. Well Stella I am writing with a Spencerian pen
No 1 and as I am not used to such a small affair I dont know as you
will be able to read this. I wish I could write as well at a desk as you
can sitting on the floor Well! I see I am drawing near the end of this
sheet and will say good bye for this time hoping to hear from you
very soon
I remain.
Your loving Norman
SWAK

Spartansburg,
June 14-1896
Dear Norman,
I guess you will think I am a good while answering your letter but if
you will forgive me this time I will try and give you a more prompt
reply next time. Dr. Seabury was here last Saturday and he thought
Pa was better but I can't see very much change in him but I guess
he is a little better. The Doctor don't want him to eat anything but
malted milk & broth or beef tea and he gets so hungry it seems a
pity that he can't eat. Lulu came out a week ago last Saturday we
went about a mile and a half from here and picked about 35 quarts
of tame strawberries I was so lame for a few days after that I walked
like an old woman. Mr. Davis (the gentleman you met when here)
and his wife stayed with us last Sunday night. I liked her very
much. They invited us to come and see them some time. Pa is awfully blue to day talks as though he never could get well and it does
seem as though he aught to begin to gain if he ever is going to.
Norman I expect you out the 4th Do you think you can get away?
Well Norman I can't think of much worth writing so please excuse
this poorly scribbled letter and write very soon.
Yours with love,
Stella
S.W.A.K.

The well-preserved village of Fredonia, about twelve miles northeast of Chautauqua Lake, looks much as it did when this letter was written.

Jamestown N.Y.
June 20, 1896
My Dear Stella,
I received you most welcome letter yesterday but have been too busy to answer it Till this afternoon, Well Stella I hope your father is better by this time. How I wish I was with you to-day. I am writing at the office and it is very warm here. I was down and stayed all night with Fred & Mattie a week ago. I had a good visit. They have things quite comfortable and I see no reason why they can't get along nicely. Mart & Edith were there also. They have finished their school and are going to move to Fredonia in a short time. He was in yesterday and paid me what he owed. I also have received what was coming from N.O. Waterman for work over a year ago. I just saw George up town. He has nearly completed the contract to purchase a farm. It is situated on the Lake road about one mile from my sisters and less than a mile from where he used to live when you was there. I am glad Lulu came out she will be such good company for you. How long does she intend to stay? Tell her if she will stay till the 4th I will be down to see her. Yes Stella! I think now if nothing happens I will come and spend the 4th of July with you I shall take the Inventory next Sat. and we will have Payday come earlier in the week as the Mill will not run that day. Last night the association Wheelmen took a run up to Mark's to Supper. we had a fine time I tell you. there was 13 of us in Line. Well my dear I see I have nearly filled the sheet so will close for this time and go and cleanup my Wheel good bye for this time and write soon to
Your loving
Norman
Excuse this envelope I am just out
SWAK

Pierce is Eliza's maiden name. Eliza grew up and married in the vicinity of Sparta where her parents still live.

Spartansburg-
June 23-1896
My Dear Norman,
I received your very welcome letter yesterday and as I am going to town to night will write you a few lines. I am very much worried about Pa again he hasn't been as well for the last two days and looks very bad. I think you must have had a very pleasant time at your sisters. Lulu is at her Grandpa Pierces now. I went after her to day but she had gone a berrying. I received a card from Irva yesterday stating that Phils little girl is dead took carbonic acid for cough syrup through mistake and died in about an hour. they had three Doctors but couldn't save her. I am so glad you can come out the 4th. I don't suppose you will enjoy yourself as well as in Jamestown but–I will a great deal better Well! the horse is waiting for me so
good by
Your loving
Stella
(S.W.K's)
P.S. I think Lulu will stay out until August.

Jamestown, N.Y.
June 25, 1896
Dear Stella,
Yours of the 23d Received to day am sorry Your Pa is not better. It does seem as though there must be a change soon, and Stella Let us hope it will be for the better. It is four weeks Sat. since I was down I believe. and I have thought every time before I would get a letter that surely it would bring news that he was better. Our Pastor spoke in Prayer meeting the other night upon the subject of Praying for the sick. I wish you might have heard him. He referred us to the last Chapter of "James" where it speaks of calling in the Elders of the Church 14th & 15th verses. Stella I wish you might have the privilege of enjoying some of

the good meetings that we have here. Sunday Afternoon at the mens meeting in the Y.M.C.A. there was a young lady of the Salvation Army spoke and she gave us an excellent address. She also spoke to a good audience at the Baptist church in the evening. She was at one time Principal of Corry High School Perhaps you may have heard of her before her name is Miss Alene Skinner. Tuesday evening another fellow and I rode to Bemus Point and back It was a very enjoyable trip it is a trifle less than 11 miles up there and we rode it in 50 min without hurry-ing. To night the Club are going to Celeron and take in the Exhibit of the Photographer's Convention which is being held there this week. I have had some thoughts of riding my wheel out but presume I will not. If I do I shall put a suit of clothes in a Satchel and send by Express. I think I could come down in 4 hours easily. I see no reason now why I cant come, on the 4th all right and possibly the day before as the factory may be closed that day also to do some repairing. I hope you do not think for a minute that I would rather stay here, or that I would enjoy myself as well here on the 4th as with you. By the way Stella we never yet spent the 4th of July together have we. Well! I see that although this is a large sheet of paper I nearly filled it so will close for this time. hoping to hear from you again before Saturday July 4th

I remain Your loving

Norman

Murdock Farm, Sparta Township, Pa.

From Irva.

Ridgway, Pa.
June 28 1896
Dear Sister Stell
I recieved your Letter a few days a go and was very Glad to
heare thar Father was some better and hope he will only continue
to get better. Phill and Nell ar out to Mishegan on a visett and I
have my hands pretty full to see to everything. Will has been most
all weak here and will go to Kane to morrow I guess he is geting
a good delivery for Aug. but he cant let liquor a lone I se that
every time he comes here that he feals pretty good I try my best to
hav him do better but I cant see as it does much good Well keep
me posted how father is I will clos hoping to here from you soon
From your Bro Irving

Spartansburg, Pa
June 30-96
Dear Norman,
I received your letter Saturday I dont know whether you will
receive this in time to answer but hope you will so I will know
whether to meet you or not. Would you have to go back on
Sunday if you come on your wheel? Pa is feeling better than
when I wrote you last. the Doctor thinks the bunch in his side is
smaller. Will came home last night guess he will stay until
Monday. I am thinking some of going to Corry if I can get away
to have some teeth filled and how I do dread it. Lulu is a great
deal of company for me I wish she could stay out longer. Well
Good by until I see you. I hope you can come out on Friday.
Yours Lovingly,
Stella

Jamestown, N.Y.
July 2, 1896
Dear Stella,
Your welcome letter recd at noon to day. I am so glad your father
is feeling better. I have decided to come on the train and if nothing happens will be down Saturday morning. I have been very
busy lately, am making up the pay-roll to day, and will pay up
tomorrow My! but this is about the warmest day we have had
this summer. but it is quite comfortable in the office with the
Mercury at 82 compared with the Spinning Room where it is 90
with 3 large fans running Well Stella I have lots to do to day so I
will not try to write very much. I will send this by the Afternoon
train and think you will get it tomorrow if anyone goes to the
Post Office.
Good by till Saturday
Your loving
Norman

Tuesday afternoon at the cotton mill. Norman has shown up for work a day late. The Fourth of July celebration at Celeron is described. Celeron is beginning its third season.

Jamestown N. Y.
July 7, -96
1 o'clock P.M.
Dear Stella,

I am home all right at last. I got here about 10-30 The train on the Erie R. R. being about 1/2 hour behind time Well Stella I don't think Mr. Smith cares a great deal if I did not get here in time. When I came in he was at my desk doing something and I said to him Well! I got back after awhile and he wanted to know how I came to miss the train and I told him there was no reason except my carelessness. then he said he was very much annoyed that I should do such a thing and that he was up nearly all night last night working at the Engine and then had to come in and see to my work too. Of course I told him I was very sorry and hoped that he would not lose confidence in me on account of this mistake. etc But you know he didn't scold at all but just sort of talked in a way that made me most wish he would give me a scolding. But as far as my work is concerned it is not crowding me a bit in fact I don't intend to do very much this afternoon as I am rather sleepy and I believe Book-keeping is just about the hardest thing there is to do when one doesn't feel wide-awake. I wish I might have just seen the crowd that was here Saturday. They say there were 13 excursions to Celeron. there was one train came in from the East with 21 coaches all filled to their utmost capacity. Sister Frances was down to see me yesterday and took dinner at my boarding place. She supposed of course that I had to be back yesterday. I may go up there this evening on my wheel if I don't feel too tired. Our machinist Mr. Hall whom I was speaking of to you this morning just came in the office and said Well! I suppose you just had a lovely time didn't you Norman and of course I told him that I did. The Mr Weidner who works here was telling me today about an Aunt of his who had a tumor and was sick a long time and reduced almost to a skeleton but recovered and is well now. he said the doctor gave her something which absorbed it without performing an operation. The way he

— 136 —

came to speak of it was his wife is very sick and I asked him about her and then told about how your father was. When I came in sight of the Lake this morning I wished you had been with me the sun was shining and one of the large Steamers was going along and altogether it was a very pretty sight I tell you Stella "Jamestown on Chaut. Lake" is a nice place to live and I hope it may be His will that it shall be our home someday.

Good by for this time Stella and write very soon to your loving Norman

S.W.A.K.

Stella's cousin Willie Ketchum is a photographer. Many family pictures bear his logo.

Spartansburg,
July 13th 1896
Dear Norman,
Your letter received Friday P.M. was glad to hear you arrived all O.K. I think if Mr. S. knew how real hard you tried to make that train he wouldn't have scolded at all. Pa is feeling about the same I guess. Dr. Seabury was here Saturday he thinks he is gaining but the bunch in his side had not grown small as fast as when here before. Well: a week ago to night at about this time I believe we were trying to keep out of the rain, What do you think there is a young man from Jamestown rakeing for us his name is Harry Jones and he smokes a pipe. says he is a machinist and works in the Bicycle shop there, and is out in the country to get fat Cousin Willie Ketchum came from Union on his wheel Sun. said he had a break down and was two or three hours fixing his wheel. I think there must have been quiet a crowd at Celeron. I would like to have been there if it had been possible, – wouldn't you? Did you tell your people how you happened to stay until Tuesday, when I came by Uncle Lon's they commenced questioning me and Lulu says Norman missed the train didn't he and of course I had to tell them you did. Lulu hasn't been here since the day you went away. Norman this is rather a dry letter but there is not very much excitment around here so guess you will have to put up with it. Pa says to tell you to keep your nose clean.

Good by
From your loving
Stella

Jamestown, N.Y.
Jul. 15, 1896
Dear Stella,
Your letter rec'd to day. I am going to be very prompt in answering it and you must do the same. Doesn't it seem good though to
know your father is gaining even if it is a little slow Yes! I told
my folks all about how I came to stay till Tuesday Morning. Miss
Williams (The lady where I board you know) said I missed it pur-
posely and I told her of course I did but that it cost me $1.33 to
do so. I dont know as I told you but of course I had to pay my
fare home which was $1.08 almost as much as the return trip tick-
ets cost me. Last Thursday night I went up to my sisters and
stayed. and last Saturday I went up to George's and stayed over
night. Then Sunday morning I went up to my Aunt's where
father lives I got up there about 8 o'clock and stayed until 5 in
the Afternoon. Do you know Stella it was the first time I had
been there since Grandma's funeral nearly a year ago that is to
stay any. Well! I have been quite busy since I came home making
out the Semi Annual Statement besides doing the other necessary
work. I almost held my breath while finishing it for fear it would
balance on the wrong side. but am glad to say it was not in fact it
was rather better than the last 6 months of last year. Just at present business is the poorest with us that is has been since I came
here. We have orders sufficient for the remainder of this week but
after that it is a blank. The mill is not going to run next Saturday
as it will be stopped for more repairs on the Engine. How I wish I
could be with you then Stella but it is rather out of the question I
suppose. To night is prayer meeting night here How I wish you
was going to be here to go. I know you would enjoy it. Well! I see
I have scribbled this sheet nearly full as usual so I will say good-
bye once more.
dont forget to write very soon to your
loving
Norman

It turns out another weekend visit was not out of the question. It has been only two weeks since Norman's last visit, and he is certainly aware that another visit so soon may not be "proper." The mill being closed on Saturday, he takes the opportunity to try the trip on his wheel.

Jamestown, N.Y.
Monday morning
Jul 20, – 96
Dear Stella,
How are you this morning. Well! I got home all right. I arrived in Corry at 15 minutes of 5 and it was sprinkling some, and looked so very rainy that I waited there for the train which left at 6-45 arriving in Jamestown at 7-45. and I was home and in bed at 9 oclock. Do you know Stella I think it was a good thing I waited as long as I did because if I had started 1/2 or 3/4 of an hour sooner I might have gotten past Corry before it looked Rainy and I would surely have been caught in the rain, as it began raining here about 6 oclock so they say. Well I thought when I got to Corry that it would be an awful long two hours to wait but I got to visit with a man there and we talked about wheels and wheel- ing and roads, etc, etc, until Supper time came and he went to supper I suppose and then I ate my lunch and then it was nearly train time. Stella! when I sat there at Corry waiting and it began to rain I thought I would have given a good deal to have been able to let you know that I was not out in it but that I was very comfortable and sure of getting home in good season But I don't believe I will start out to make such a long trip again with the intentions of returning on Sunday for somehow I cant make it seem quite the right thing to do Mr. Smith got his face scalded this morning with steam I dont know how badly as I was at breakfast at the time. I just met him going to his breakfast as I came from mine and it looked very bad. Tell your father that I have not forgotten about the peaches that he was wishing for and when I go up town I will see what I can do about it. Well Stella I guess I had better draw this to a close and go to work for Thomas Henry,
Write very soon to your loving,
Norman.
Good bye,

Mr. Harrington is the father of Stella's friend, Ida. Norman missed Eliza when she passed through Jamestown the previous August (letters July 31; Aug. 24, 1895).

Spartansburg, Pa.
July 22–1896
Wednesday P.M.
Dear Norman.
Your very very welcome letter received yesterday. I am so glad you were so fortunate as not to get caught in the rain How I did long to know just where you was and what you would do when it commenced to rain Sunday night! I think it was a good thing it rained so you had to take the train for I think it was too much of a trip for you so soon after the one you took the day before. I think Pa is a little better than he was Sunday but don't feel very good. Mr. Harrington borrowed an invalids chair for him so I am in hopes he can sit up more and maybe he will gain faster. I took Will to the train yesterday he is going to Union to canvass I expect him home again Saturday night. Dot's back bothers her so she can hardly get around and so it just keeps me a hustleing most of the time. I did quite a washing to day and am very tired but thought I would try and scribble you a few lines. Norman you don't know how I hated to see you go away but I was very glad to have you come as of course you know. John returned from the burg a little while ago and brought the peaches. The most of them were nearly spoiled but Pa can eat some of them. I think they must have been lovely when you sent them and he is very very thankful to you for them. Well! Norman it is now after 9 o'clock and since I commenced this letter Pa has been feeling very bad but is easier now I received a letter from Irva and he writes that Eliza may come out the last of this or first of next week. I wish you might see her this time but I don't suppose you will. Tell Thomas Henry I am very sorry he scalded his face. No you need not neither but I am just the same. Well! I believe it is about my usual bed-time So Good night for this time and write very soon to your loving friend,
Stella Murdock
S.W.A.K.

Jamestown, N.Y.
July 27, 1896
Monday Afternoon
My Dear Stella, –
I recd your as ever welcome letter Saturday And am just stealing time this P.M. to answer it. I worked Sat Afternoon In fact I have been very busy all the time last week. Mr. Smith is sending out a circular letter to his Batting Customers and it makes lots of work for me directing envelopes etc. Saturday morning I took about 300 of them up to the Post Office. I have not seen any of my folks since I came home, it having rained nearly every day so that the roads are too muddy to ride my wheel. I went to church twice yesterday and to The Men's meeting at the Y.M.C.A. in the afternoon. Stella I wish you might have heard the Sermon that I did yesterday morning I tell you I think it would be a very hard hearted person who could listen to such a talk and not be inspired to do better. Tell your father I am glad to hear about the invalid chair and hope he may be able to use it a great Deal. Has Eliza come out yet? How I wish I might see her but unless she is going to stay quite a long time I suppose I shall not this time. I have an invitation to a reception tonight given to the officers and committeemen of the Y.M.C.A. by Mr & Mrs Wm H Proudfit one of the leading clothiers of the city. It was to have been held at their summer cottage near the lake about 4 miles out of town but since it has rained nearly all day I think perhaps it will be in the Association Rooms instead. There is to be a concert in the Baptist Church tomorrow Eve by the Chaut Lake Concert Company under the Auspices of the Young Peoples Society. Stella I just wish you could be there. and now I shall have to say good-bye for this time if this is more dull than usual you must excuse it for my head is aching to beat the Band. Write very soon to your same old fellow.
Norman
"S.W.A.K."

Spartansburg, Pa
Aug 3d '96
Monday P.M.
My Dear Norman, –
I will now answer your very welcome letter which I received a
few days ago. Well Norman the Doctors have now decided that
Pa will have to have an operation they say the bunch has quit
growing smaller. I look for Doctor Seabury here to day and then I
suppose they will set the day. O it is such a terrible thing to think
of but I believe it is the last resort and can only hope and pray for
the best. The Doctors seem to think he stands a good chance to
go through with it all right. Eliza is here now she brought her
wheel and I have been trying to ride it some I dont know how
long she will be out but I guess not more than two or three weeks
I would like very much to have you come out but you know best
whether you can or not. We have a hired girl has been here just a
week and I suppose will be my sister-in-law how is that for getting accquainted quick. I suppose Will will stay at home this fall
and winter now. I suppose some one wouldn't like it if they
knew I told. Norman I don't know as I ought to have written this
be sure and not tell any one for Pa didn't want me to tell. Dot
and Eliza are going to the burg and I havn't much time to write
so if you can't make it out just let me know and I will do better
next time. Good by for this time and write very soon to your loving Stella.

Jamestown N.Y.
Aug 5, 1896
Wednesday, P.M.
Dear Stella,
I just received your letter at dinner time and will take the pleasure of answering immediately. I cant tell you how sorry I am
that it is going to be necessary for your father to undergo an
operation but as you say we can only hope and pray that it may
be a succesful one. you forgot to tell me in your letter how he is
feeling but I suppose about the same as he has. My! but arent we
having warm weather though. you must be careful and not try to

ride Eliza's wheel too far this hot weather or it may make you sick. I suppose Derwood and Mate are both out with her, How I wish I might see them all. I was up to my sisters and stayed night before last they are all well as usual and report George's folks the same. none of them had heard of my being down to your place the last time and it had been so rainy ever since I came back that I had not been up that way. I am much busier lately than I was a few weeks ago but I am glad of it for the time goes faster on that account. Mr Smith Jr. is coming home from Eng. the last of this month I am glad to say and then it will be easier for me to get away. The concert I wrote you was going to be held in the Baptist Church was a success financially at last the profits being a little over $50. I suppose by this time you have plenty of ripe apples. they are very plenty and cheap here. Well Stella I cant think of very much that is interesting to write but I know that if my letters are to you as yours are to me you will be glad to get it any way. How I wish I could see you this Afternoon but can only ask you to write very soon and all the particulars about your father. I remain as ever
Yours lovingly & Prayerfully
Norman.
"S W A K"

Lexington Heights Hospital
Buffalo, N.Y.
August 12 1896
Dear Norman: –
Pa and I came here yesterday Dr. Seabury came with us, we started from home at about 2 o'clock A.M. and got in Buffalo at about eight o'clock. Pa stood the trip splendid much better than I expected we took the sleeper and he slept nearly all the way from Corry. They expect to operate on him Friday I do dread it so but I think it is his only chance of recovery. It is very nice here at the hospital and he has excellent care and I am allowed to be with him all the time through the day if I wish. I take my meals here but as they are all full I have to take lodging out have a room about two blocks from here it seems rather strange not to have to

be working all the time. I took a long walk this morning. I expect to stay about a week if Pa gets along all right. He is very much pleased with the nurses and I guess he has about the pleasantest room in the house. Irva came out the night before we left. Well! Good by for this time and write very soon from your loving
Stella

Jamestown N.Y.
August 14, 1896
My Dear Stella,
You may imagine I was some surprized to find when I went home to dinner a letter from you with a Buffalo Post-mark on it But you dont know how glad I am that your father can be where he is and my prayer is that the Physicians that attend him may be given Wisdom and skill from on high and that it may be God's will that he shall recover Stella I wish I could be with you. It seems as though Irva had ought to be with you and although you said nothing about it perhaps he is going to be. When I came from dinner to day there was a crowd of people about the railroad crossing and I found that a little girl had had her foot crushed under a train I dont know how badly as they took her right to the hospital. I hope it is not so hot in Buffalo as it is in some of the large cities and I suppose it is not on acct of its being so near the lake. Well Stella I am very busy this afternoon and so I will close, and go and take this to the Post Office and I think you will get it to night tell your father to keep good courage and all will be well and Stella write me just as soon as you can for I shall hardly be able to wait till I hear from you. Good bye for this time. and may God's blessing be with you both.
Yours as ever
Norman

*Pa dies. His funeral is held on the farm followed by a burial in the local ceme-
tery conducted by the Odd Fellows. This letter is written after Norman's con-
dolence visit.*

Jamestown, N.Y.
August 20, 1896
1 p.m.
Dear Stella,
I will now take the pleassure of writing you a few lines. How are
you feeling by this time? I hope you have been able to get rested
some. I arrived in good time yesterday and found plenty waiting
for me to do, but I can assure you I did very little work yesterday.
I did not realize how tired I was until I got here and tried to
apply my-self to my work which it was nearly impossible for me
to do. Mr. Smith did not say a word in regard to my coming back
sooner than I did and I think it would have been all right if I had
stayed till last night. I went to prayer meeting last evening but I
am afraid it did me very little good as I had to fight to keep
awake. Stella you don't know how I hated to come and leave you
this time. It just seems as though I could not be reconciled to it. I
wonder if it is wrong for me to feel thus about it. I suppose it is
all for the best but how hard it is to always think that. As things
look now I think the Cotton Mill may have to shut down for a
few weeks. of course I hate to see it stop but if it does I shall be
glad to have a little vacation although I can ill afford it. and I
think you can guess where and with whom I would want to
spend the greater part of it. If nothing happens I shall go up to
George's next Saturday I have not been up there in quite a long
time. O Stella! I realize it is almost impossible for even those who
are very near freinds to say anything that is really comforting in
such a time as this but I am going to remind you of that verse in
Isaaih 41-10 "Fear not for I am with thee be not dismayed for I
am thy God. I will strengthen thee; yea! I will help thee. yea! I
will uphold thee with the right hand of my Righteousness" and
now my darling good bye for this time and write very soon to
your loving
Norman

Spartansburg, Pa.
Aug 25th
Tuesday Morning
Dear Norman,
Your as ever welcome letter recd a few days ago. What beautiful
weather we are having. I stayed over to Uncle Lon's Saturday
night and have been to the burg or some place nearly every day
since you were here It is so lonesome in the house that I cant bear
to stay here Norman you dont know nor never will until you
have the same experience how hard it is to have those whom we
love so much taken from us and still I feel that I have a great deal
to be thankful for. How much different I feel about it than I
would if he had been taken a year ago. Do you think the Mill will
be shut-down. I hope you will have a little vacation if it is. I was
at Britton Run to church last evening and heard an excellent sermon. There is a meeting there every night this week except
Saturday evening Eliza and Irva have both gone. When can you
come out? I am thinking some of going down to Uncle Lon Grays
on an errand but may not go until to-morrow so I guess I had
better close for this time and find out. Good by from
Your loving Stella.

Norman to visit again. He trusts the etiquette of mourning does not apply.

Jamestown, N.Y.
Aug-27-96
Thur. P.M.
Dear Stella,
I just received your letter at dinner time and am glad to write
and tell you I have decided to come down to see you next Sat.
Aug 29th but as it is Payday I will not be able to come till the
evening train, I hope you may get this so that you can meet me. I
suppose some people would say it is too soon to come down
again but somehow I don't feel that way about it. Last Saturday I
was up to Georges' and stayed over night they are all well except
himself and I hope nothing serious is the matter of him but he
didn't eat scarcely anything while I was there. I am afraid he is

working too hard. Yes! we are having lovely weather. it makes me think of those days in the grape country. how I would like to be there again for a few days but I don't expect I shall be. Last night was Prayer meeting we had an excellent service I am glad that you can attend meeting. I wonder if we cant go to church next Sunday, Well! Stella I can't think of much that is interesting to write so I will close for this time
Your loving
Norman.

Tuesday afternoon at the mill. Norman has visited Sparta seven times since his proposal.

Jamestown. N.Y.
Sept 1st 1896
1:00 P.M.
My Dear Stella,
I will now give you a few minutes of my time and let you know that I arrived safely. My! but aren't we having cool weather lately though? I had to have the steam in the office on this morning for quite a while. I had quite a visit with Elder Stone on the train yesterday he seems like a very nice man. he told me that he had a nephew working in one of the factories here and that he would like to have me get acquainted with him. but when he told me his name it was a fellow whom I know quite well as he attended the Business College at the same time I did and is a member of the Y.M.C.A. I didn't tell you that I came very near losing $10 last Saturday. Well! it was like this I never have been in the habit of counting the money I get for the Pay-Roll until I get back to the office. and last Saturday it was ten dollars short. I of course knew that I had not lost it coming for I had it in my Satchel. but it was quite a different thing to make the people at the Bank know it too and said they could not make it good unless they found they had $10 too much when they took Cash Balance Well! you can imagine how glad I was when I got home and Mr. Smith told me that they found it and I had not lost it. When I was up there yesterday I went in and talked to the President about it and he said I should always count it before I left there and that I might come in

his office to do it when there was not room outside. I see I am nearing the limit of the sheet and as I have lots to do will say good-bye for this time
write very soon
Yours lovingly,
Norman.
"S.W.A.K"

The farm continues to function without Pa Murdock. Three weeks after her father's death, Stella is clearly distracted.

Spartansburg, Pa.
Sep. 8-'96
Tuesday Evening
Dear Norman,
How do you do this evening? I would much rather have a visit with you than to be writing. We have had the thrashers here to-day and so it has been quite a busy day with us. Will came back a week ago to-day he went away yesterday canvassing. Rilla is here with us. I was quite surprised on returning from church Sunday to find Dr. Seabury here he only stayed until the next morning and I took him and Will to the train they came very near missing it did not have to hitch the horse even. Well this is interesting to you I don't think. I have been thinking some to day of going to the grape country but guess I wont What do you think about it? I think it would be too much like work. I intend to take the morning train for Corry guess I will not come back until Saturday I am going to have my teeth filled pulled or something done to them My! but I do dread it. I don't know yet how we are going to live here this winter but I think the way things look now that I had better stay here until Spring. There is to be a Fred Silver speech at Britton Run this evening but I thought I didn't care anything about hearing it. Dot says to give you her best wishes. Well! Good night for this time & write very soon
From Your loving friend
Stella Murdock
S.W.A.K.

Norman has concerns about his younger brother, Floyd, who is mentioned only in passing in the collected correspondence. It appears Floyd is under his father's care.

Jamestown, N.Y.
Sep 10, 1896
My Dear Stella,
How are you this afternoon. I hope well. I received your letter today and suppose you are in Corry to day from what you wrote. I hope that the dentist may let you off easily. My! but aren't we having lovely weather though? It makes me half wish that I was working out of doors and then I think of the cold cold winter that will soon be here and am thankful that I have such a good place. I have not seen any of my folks since I came back but suppose they are all well or I would have heard from them. To day is Floyd's birthday, he is 14 I think. how short a time it seems to me now looking back since he was a little fellow in dresses about like Frankie was. and then he was so sick and we thought we would lose him. and now I can not help thinking – but no! I won't say it because I know better and I only hope and pray that he may grow up a good man. Well! Stella it seems to me that if I have got to wait for you until Spring, it will be the longest winter I ever knew. but I suppose like all before it, it will soon pass. I am willing to leave it for you to decide and if it seems to you the right way I will wait and try to be patient. But somehow since your father has been taken away from us I feel so different about you and Stella when I think how lonely you are with out him it just seems as though I couldn't bear to have you away from me so long. I think now if all goes well I will come down one week from next Saturday if you are going to be at home. and if I do will write you early next week so that you may know for sure. good bye for this time
and write very soon
I am as ever yours
Norman Ingerson

Stella's meaning is unclear. Probably, she saw Uncle Siles from Jamestown at Mrs. Baker's dinner party.

Spartansburg,
Sept 15 '96.
Dear Norman –
I rec'd your very welcome letter Saturday evening am glad you intend coming out next Sat. hope to hear from you before so that I will know for sure. Well! the Dentist didn't kill me quite but have to go back Friday to have a tooth filled so perhaps I hadn't better brag. I was at Mrs. Bakers (Dots sister) Uncle Siles and took dinner with Mrs. Wales (Pa's cousin) while there in Corry. My! but wasn't it warm last week it seems good to have it cooler again. Rilla is up to Mr. Millards and so Dot and I are alone most of the time of course the hired men are here I guess Dot and I will go to town to-night – Norman I can't think of any thing worth writing so you must excuse this horrid letter this time and write very soon.
Truly Yours,
Stella
Dot says remember me to Norman.

Jamestown, N.Y.
Sep 15, 1896
Dear Stella,
I am glad to say I will be down next Saturday if nothing happens on the evening train. I will not write much in this letter but hope to say a great deal when I see you. I had my picture taken last Saturday and they promised to have them finished before next Sat.
Good bye for this time
Your loving
Norman

The date for the wedding discussed, to be settled in the next letter. Norman eagerly undertakes preparations. Always someone is sick. This time it is Aunt Lucinda Gray whom Norman probably saw on his just completed visit.

Jamestown N.Y.
Sep. 22, 1896
1. O'Clock P.M.
Dear Stella,
How do you do this afternoon, My! but this is a cold dreary day out for Sep. I have had the steam on in the office quite a bit of the time to day. I reached here about ten yesterday and was just going from the station when I met Mother and Frances. she "Mother" took the train at 12-20 P.M. for Illinois. She doesnt seem to know anything about how long she will stay. but I think perhaps it will be two or three months at least. Last night I saw an Ad in the paper for some rooms for rent just a short distance from where I board and as I had nothing else to do after supper I went and looked at them just to sort of get an idea how much it was going to cost. I found they were 6 large rooms and a hall. they were up stairs though and they asked $5 per month for them. What do you think about living upstairs? I of course would rather live down stairs but think We could get better rooms for the same money upstairs and you know it doesnt make much more work because the water and gas of course would be in. I have been thinking to day that maybe if I found some place that suited I would take it even a few weeks before we wanted it and be sure and have no trouble about it. Well Stella! I hope you feel well satisfied about our being married this fall as I do. I enclose a leaflet describing the Y.M.C.A. Lecture Course for this winter and I am so glad that you can go to them all except probably the first one on Nov. 6. (God willing.) And now I want to say in regard to the day that Saturday Nov. 7 and 21st are pay days at the Cotton Mill and I can get away for a few days a great deal better during a week following Pay day. but of course if it makes any difference to you I can get away any time. I have not found out yet about the cost of the lettering on that Monument as I said I would but will try and do so before writing again. When you write dont forget to tell me how your Aunt Lucinda is and write very soon to your loving
Norman

— 151 —

Two Victorian ladies drive the horse and buggy to Corry.

Spartansburg, Pa.
Sept 30-96
Dear Norman,
I am quite well I thank you and how are you? Dot and I drove to
Corry yesterday and didn't get killed either but we had quite a
rainy time of it did not get home until about 9 o'clock and John
was gone and had to put out the horse myself and in the dark at
that as Dot could not find the lantern for a long time. We stopped
at Aunt Lucindas yesterday. She does not seem to gain very fast
says she is discouraged. I think she is a pretty sick woman. Uncle
Lon is going to have our sale a week from Tues. In regard to our
having rooms up stairs I think if you can get them cheaper than
you can down perhaps you had better take them. I think it would
not make much difference in the winter whether we lived up
stairs or down but of course it would be pleasanter downstairs in
the Summer I think but use your own judgement you said the
ones you looked at were large rooms but did not tell what kind
of rooms I suppose two or three of them were bedrooms wasn't
they. I think the day will be Nov. 25. Will that suit you? I went
over to Uncle Albert Grays last Sunday My Aunt Addie Hide &
her husband were there and I had a good visit Idie my cousin
had gone to Panama Rocks on his wheel so I did not see him Well
it doesn't do anything but rain and how lonesome it is. I will
close for this time
Write very soon to your loving friend
Stella

Jamestown
Oct 2-96
Dear Stella,
Yours of Sep 30 at hand and of course welcome. I am sorry to
hear that your Aunt Lucinda gets along so slowly. I think you
must have had a very bad day to drive to Corry. My! but hasn't it
been rainy for the past week though? I have not been up the Lake
since I came from Sparta last but am thinking some of going up

to George's tomorrow. Well Stella! I have rented our future home and I am sure it will suit you. It is not upstairs. There is a kitchen, dining room, sitting room and two bedrooms besides a pantry. There is also a good cellar and the location is fine it being about the same distance from the Cotton Mill as the place where I am boarding but nearer to town and in a much better part of the City. It is a corner house with a veranda facing each street There is a family living in the rooms at present they are nice people and I don't think will leave the rooms in very bad condition. It is not a very large house and the rooms are of course not very large, but large enough I think. You will understand that we are to have just the rooms downstairs. There is a family living upstairs but as there is an outside stairway for them to use I don't think they will interfere with us at all. We will begin to pay rent from November 1st and it is to be $8 per month the water rent being paid by the man who owns the house. I tell you I wish you could see this house Stella It is a great deal better than I had any idea I could get for the money. I only regret that we cannot occupy it sooner, in fact I was hoping you would set the day in the first part of the month rather than the last but I suppose you could not get ready much sooner. Yes! Nov. 25 suits me all right if it does you.

Did you mean that the sale was going to be one week from Tuesday Sep 29 or one week from next Tuesday? I wrote a letter to the clerk of the courts at Meadville and asked him if it would be necessary for both of us to come there in order to obtain a license and found it is only necessary for me to go. Well Stella I must draw this to a close. I think I will come down the last part of this month or first of next excuse this poorly scribbled epistle and write very soon

Yours lovingly,

Norman W. Ingerson

S.W.A.K.

The farm sale is planned. The hired men say their goodbyes. Norman is making inquiries about the inscription for Pa's marker.

Spartansburg, Pa.
Oct. 8th 1896.
Dear Norman –
Your letter received a few days ago and as I intend going to town to day guess I will write you a few lines first. Will is at home now has been home for a week and intends staying until after the Sale which is next Tuesday he is going to move to DuBois has rented a house right near where I was. Rilla is out there now and he has shipped his goods. he has made it very unpleasant for us since he came home and I will be glad when he goes back. Isn't it awful for me to write such about my brother? When you write again write about the lettering on that monument Irva may come out to the Sale and I would like to know before then, I am glad you are so well suited with the house you have rented. I am very glad that I concluded not to stay here all winter for I don't think it would be necessary and I am sure not very pleasant I was at church last Sunday Elder Black preached such a good sermon. Roger was over Sunday and bid us Good by he went Monday Russ H. went with him. Dot's cousins in Oil City have been visiting her this last week. Well Norman I don't think of much to write and don't know as you will be able to read what I have written.
Good Bye for this time and write very soon to your loving,
Stella.

Jamestown N.Y
Oct 11, 1896
Dear Stella,
Your letter received yesterday. found me well as usual excepting a severe cold. I went up to Sisters last night and stayed, went on my wheel and came back this morning, and as I was too late to go to church, and knowing I shall be very busy tomorrow, I thought I had better write you today. one week ago yesterday I went up to George's on the train, found Kate was at Mayville

visiting her mother the next day George and I drove up there and I came home from there on the train in the evening. I had a real good visit. As to the lettering on that monument the man I saw here a Mr. Cook said they charge 5 a letter for common lettering on marble and from 10 to 15 for raised letter this is their price when they go to the Cemetery here and do it. I told him to write to your uncle Lon about it. If Irva comes out tell him I would like to have him come back this way and stop in Jamestown if he can. Stella I think you had better put your stove up for sale Tues don't you? Well Stella the days are going by very slowly to me I think I now shall come down in 3 weeks. It seemed like a long time to look ahead. By the way! I was in the other day and got measured for a suit it will cost me 30 dollars. don't you think I am extravagant though? Frances & Kate want us to come there for Thanksgiving either at one place or the other. I told them I didn't know but that it should be as you said. I have been thinking Stella that when I come down I might bring my trunk and when we do come to Jamestown anything you could put in it would come as baggage and save so much Freight. Well I see I have exhausted the sheet with my scribbling and will close for this time. write very soon to your loving
Norman

Spartansburg, Pa.
Oct-22-1896.
Thursday Evening
Dear Norman,
I guess you will think I am quite a while answering your letter. How is your cold by this time? I haven't been feeling very well lately. Irva did not come out. I was very sorry for I did want to see him. Things did not sell very good, the sorrel colts went for $120 and they bid so low on the other horses that they did not let them go at all. I could not put my stove up for Dot has to have it here this winter. She seems to wish now that I was not going away so soon but its too late now isn't it? I shall look for you out a week from Saturday shall I? It seems like quite a while since you were here. If you think you could put your trunk on the back

of our little buggy perhaps you had better bring it. We only have
the one buggy to go with now. If it would trouble you any to
bring it I wouldn't for I don't think it would save very much but
maybe it would. I don't know. I received a letter from Dollie
Gray, she was in the grape country said she thought it would be
her first and last season in the vineyard said she had been in
three different places since she went there don't think she was as
lucky as we were do you? I can tell better when I see you where
we will be spending Thanksgiving. It is now past bed-time and
so I will close hoping to hear from you soon.
Yours lovingly,
Stella.

Jamestown, N.Y.
Oct 26, 1896
Monday morning
Dear Stella,
I received your letter Saturday, I am very sorry that you are not
feeling well. I do hope you will not be sick. Doesn't it seem good
though to have it so nice and pleasant after such a lot of rainy
weather.
Yesterday was such a lovely day. I went to a bible class at the
Y.M.C.A. at 9:15 A.M. and then to church at 10:45. A Mr. Wells
who is asst Sec. of the Y.M.C.A. took dinner with me. Then we
attended a meeting at 4 o'clock and the Epworth League at 6 and
then went to preaching service at the Baptist Church at 7 don't
you think that was filling the day pretty full of meetings? Well
Stella I told Mr. Smith this morning and there will be no trouble
about my getting away for as long as I need to. I am coming
down next Sat. on the morning train. O! I am so glad for I tell
you the last five weeks have seemed very long to me. You may
tell Dot that I don't blame her any for wishing you was going to
stay longer but that she may come and visit us as much as she
pleases. Well Stella, as it is time for me to go to dinner I will draw
this to a close hoping to see you Saturday.
Yours with love
Norman.

The 1896 election. The Republicans take over. Norman has spent the weekend in Sparta.

Jamestown, N.Y.
Nov 4th 1896
Wed: morning
Dear Stella,
How are you this morning? Well! Election is over and McKinley will be our next President I suppose. Jamestown just went wild last night. the excitement was so intense, I was up town till after midnight, therefore I am feeling sort of "bummy" to day. They say there never was so much interest exhibited at an election in this town before, almost the total vote being cast by noon. Well! Stella you will see I have sent you 25 dollars instead of 15 of course if you dont need it all to use now it will undoubtedly come handy sometime. Did you send by Mr Snodgrass for your cloak? I wrote to Elder Black yesterday and enclosed a directed envelope for reply, I think I shall hear from him soon. have you done anything about the organ-box yet? The box of canned fruit has not come yet. I am sort of anxious to know how long it takes it as we can tell by that some thing about how long our other stuff will be on the way. I have not seen any of my folks since I came back but think I will go up that way Saturday. Well Stella! I really can't think of much that is interesting to write. so I will say good bye for this time.
write very soon to your as ever loving
Norman
S.W.A.K.

Ingerson Residence, 314 Lincoln Street, Ca.1920.

Spartansburg, Pa.
Nov. 9-96
Dear Norman: –
I received your letter Saturday also the check havn't been down
yet to get it cashed. I will not need to use it all now but I guess it
will not come a miss when we come to get what we need Uncle
Lon is here now and he said he went and saw Brockway and he
said it would not be necessary for you to go to Meadville he said
that Uncle Lon can get it for you and all that is necessary is to
know your age and residence. Uncle Lon thought I had better
write to you first and see if you wanted him to get it. I told him I
was most sure you would. He said it would take about a week
after he sent in the application. So you answer this just as soon as
you get it. Pa's cousin Vinton Murdock was buried yesterday
funeral was at Britton Run M.E. church he died in a hospital we
did not know he was sick until he was brought to the burg a
corpse. Mr & Mrs Davis was out yesterday to the funeral and
they want us to come and see them so if you don't have to go up
to Meadville & Uncle Lon says you don't have to couldn't you
come out Sat instead of Mon & if the roads should be good then
may be we could drive out here Sunday. Uncle Lon is waiting so
will close
Good by & write soon
Your loving – Stella.

*This and Stella's answer to the previous letter crossed in the mail. The address
of the house to which Norman takes his bride is 300 Lincoln Street. Norman's
boss, Mr. T.H. Smith, lives a block away at 500 East Sixth Street. The "Darrah
House," named for Mr. Smith's daughter, Jessie Smith Darrah, to whom it was
willed, is one of Jamestown's best preserved Victorian buildings. Today it is
owned by the architectural firm of Harrington and Sandberg. Norman enclosed
the following note with his letter:*

Centerville, Penn'a
Nov. 4 1896
Mr. N.W. Ingerson
Dear Sir,
I will comply with your request to perform your marriage cere-
mony on the 25th with pleasure.
Yours very truly,
J.F. Black

Jamestown, N.Y
Nov 9-96
Monday Morn
Dear Stella,
Don't be frightened at getting this. The first letter I ever wrote
you without first receiving an answer to the previous one. How
do you do this fine morning? don't we have just lovely weather
though for November? Well! Stella we are not going to live in the
house I had rented the man hated to move so bad that I took him
up at his offer of $5.00 and I have rented rooms on the opposite
corner of the street at seven dollars per month water rent paid,
and rent to begin the fifteenth instead of the first of the month.
There is just as much room excepting that the Kitchen & Dining
room will be one and the rooms are just as nice as the others for
all that I can see. There is a family living upstairs in the house the
same as in the other. The box of canned fruit came through Wed
night and I put it in the cellar Friday Afternoon so you see we
have taken possession already. My! but wouldn't it be nice if this
weather should continue 3 weeks more? I went up to Sisters Sat.
afternoon on my wheel and then up to George's yesterday morning returning home just at dark last night, the roads were fine but
it was very cold. Frances's children both have the whooping
cough and as George's have not had it, it may break up our little
reunion Thanksgiving day, but I decided with them that we
would go to George's anyhow and Frances & Mark will come
there if possible. Kate's mother is with her at present and will
stay until the 25th when she intends to go home and let Ada

Cobb come down as she wanted to be at home herself on Thanksgiving day and Ada had expressed a desire to be down there. Well! I guess I have scribbled about enough for this time so will close,
write very soon to your loving Norman.

Jamestown N.Y.
Nov 11, 1896
My Dear Stella,
Yours of the 9th inst just received, I am only too glad that I dont have to go to Meadville. I am sorry he (your uncle Lon) thought it necessary to wait to hear from me before making the application. Yes! I will try and come down a week from Saturday but of course I cant come until the evening train. I have told them about it over to my boarding place Frances told me she thought I ought to tell them as they might then have a chance to get someone in my place and after thinking it over I decided it was the better way. I received a letter from mother yesterday she says they have had about ten inches of snow out there. She doesnt talk as though she intended to come home for quite a while. I finished paying for my suit last Saturday so I am out of debt again and if I dont have to go to Meadville, what money I will have next payday will go quite a way toward paying our expenses week after next. Well Stella! I wrote you about all the news I could think of last Monday so I will close for this time hoping I may receive another letter from you very soon.
I am as ever
Your loving Norman.
P.S. Excuse this envelope as I am just out and dont know as I can get up town to buy any before the train goes that I want to send it by.
"S.W.A.K."

Jamestown, N.Y.
Nov. 17, 1896
1 o'clock P.M. Tuesday
Dear Stella,

How do you do today? I thought maybe I had better write you once more before coming down. I am coming sure on the evening train Saturday. I do hope that the License will come all right for I don't want to go to Medville if I can possibly avoid it. Mr. Smith knows that I intend coming away on Saturday so that it is all right as far as he is concerned but I promised to try and get back if possible sometime during Friday the 27th. I have not seen any of my folks since I wrote you last but I expect George down with the stove etc. someday this week. I went up and paid the rent last Saturday and the people said they expected to move out yesterday or today. If George comes down with the stove soon enough I will have the burner put in and ready to be fired up as soon as we may arrive. My! but this is warm weather for the time of year isn't it? How I hope it may be nice next week too.
Well Stella! I really havn't much of interest to write so I will say good-bye until Saturday Evening when I hope I may see you at the train to meet me.
I am as ever
Your loving
Norman

Stella's response to Norman's letter of November 11. She has not yet received his letter of November 17. He arrived in Sparta on Saturday evening, November 21. It appears from his reference to Mr. Smith in his last letter that he stayed with Stella in Sparta until Thursday morning, the day after the wedding, when they left for Jamestown.

Spartansburg Pa.
Thursday
Dear Norman: –
I suppose you are looking for a letter from me so I will just drop you a few lines. I did not know I was going to town until a few minutes ago and so havn't time to write much. I am looking for you out Sat. Uncle Lon said he would see about my organ I

havn't seen him since to speak to him but guess he will see to it
all right. I intend to stop there when I go over. Your last letter
was miss sent and I did not get it until Friday and Uncle Lon sent
in the application Sat. I suppose said he would and of course did.
Well good by until Sat. evening
excuse the lead pencil
Yours in haste –
Stella.

*Norman and Stella were married at the Murdock farm. Uncle Lon
and Aunt Jennie Murdock, Dot, and the Reverend J.F. Black
comprised the wedding party.*

Stella, Ca. 1925.

Epilogue

The Reverend J.F. Black married Norman and Stella on Wednesday evening, November 25, 1896, at the Sparta farm. The ceremony took place in the formal parlor with Dot, Aunt Jennie Murdock, and Uncle Lon Murdock the only guests. After spending their wedding night at the farm, the couple departed early the next morning for their rented rooms at 300 Lincoln Avenue in Jamestown. Norman and Stella took Thanksgiving dinner that night with the Ingerson family at George and Kate's farm.

Norman worked at the cotton mill for another year and a half while Stella joined the First Baptist Church. Together, they attended church events, concerts, YMCA lectures, and visited often with friends and family. Dot eventually sold the Sparta farm and moved to Jamestown. Irva and Eliza pressed on at the American Artists Alliance, but Irva's heart wasn't in the business. His interests had turned westward to the Dakotas, where he and Durwood planned to stake a claim. Will skipped from job to job in Dubois and started a new family with the former hired girl, now his wife, Lella.

Norman and Stella's first child, Franklin Irving Ingerson, was born on April 29, 1898. He died in infancy. Shortly after the baby's death, Norman and George bought out the Hollenbeck Brothers Grocery on East Third Street in Jamestown. Norman resigned from the cotton mill, and George and Kate moved to Jamestown where their family would grow to nine children. The new business incorporated in 1899 as the Ingerson Grocery Company.

Dorothy May Ingerson was born on January 7, 1900, and Marian Estelle on April 21, 1903. By 1905, the Ingerson brothers had not only expanded their original shop but also acquired a second store on East Ninth Street. Success permitted Norman and Stella to purchase a sprawling Victorian house at 314 Lincoln Street. In January, 1906, George sold his share of the company to J.W. Doubleday, proprietor of the Empire Worsted Mills in Jamestown.

In September, 1907, shortly before their eleventh wedding anniversary and thirty-fifth birthdays, Norman and Stella traveled to Toronto for the World's Fair. They left their daughters under the care of their Dubois cousins, Lulu and Mate. While in Toronto, Norman suffered a severe attack of appendicitis. Following two operations in Toronto General Hospital, he died on September 25, 1907. George traveled to Toronto to accompany Stella and Norman's body back to Jamestown. The funeral was held in the parlor of their home on Lincoln Street.

Deep in mourning, Stella's first instinct was to follow Irva to Hot Springs, South Dakota, where he and Durwood had acquired property. Irva advised against the move, so she remained with the children in Jamestown. After Norman's estate was settled, Ingerson Grocery was reorganized. The company's stock was divided into shares, and Stella was named, with George and Kate, first-year director. George resumed daily operations of the business. By 1916, despite the company's prosperous appearance, Stella's share of the profits began to decline. To make ends meet, she took in washing and ironing. A draft of a legal letter among Stella's papers indicates that George had been drawing more from the accounts than his share of salary and profits. It appears that legal action was never pursued. Stella left the company and never recovered from the financial hardship.

Upon graduation from high school, Dorothy moved to Arlington, Virginia. She worked at the Pentagon and on December 18, 1920, married Harvey H. Perry. Marian entered Battle Creek College, Battle Creek, Michigan, in 1924. She became a dietician and married William Frederick Riesmeyer, Jr. in 1929. Stella lived in the Lincoln Street house until 1925 when she moved to Arlington under the guise of helping out with Dorothy's two children. Letters from Marian at college, however, indicate that Stella was in poor health. A few months before her fifty-fourth birthday, Stella died from pancreatic cancer. She was buried beside Norman in Jamestown's Lakeview Cemetery.